UNCOMMON SENSE

*The Fight to Fix Your Workplace Culture
in the Wild West of Business*

MEL BLACKWELL

Uncommon Sense: The Fight to Fix Your Workplace Culture in the Wild West of Business

Written by Mel Blackwell

Design and cover art by Peaceful Profits.

Paperback ISBN: 978-1-967587-96-4
eBook ISBN: 978-1-967587-97-1
Hardcover ISBN: 978-1-967587-98-8

This book is a work of nonfiction. It represents the accuracy of the events mentioned to the best of the author's recollection. Some names in the book have been replaced to maintain the privacy of certain individuals.

Dedication

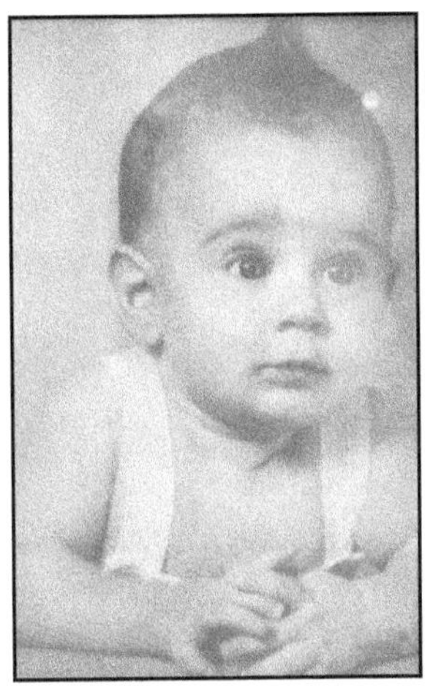

This was my mother's favorite photo of me. It is also one of my wife and kids' favorites.

This book is dedicated to my mother, Glenda Moseley Potts, who passed away a few years ago. Mom said I never took a nap, ever. I slept like a rock all night, and then I got up and hit the ground running. I could walk and climb early. I could get out of my baby crib way too early. I could climb and reach the top of every cabinet. Mom told the story many times how while at a wellness checkup with my pediatrician when I was 2 years old, she asked him if it was normal for a child to be like me. She even asked if there is anything he recommended giving me as a prescription. Per Mom's telling of the story, the pediatrician smiled and told her he would not give me anything, but joked that he had something he could prescribe for her. He then went on to further state that "He is fine. Let him grow up, and he will make you proud." She told this story many times over the years, right up until she was on her death bed. I could tell she was proud, and yet she always reminded me to keep working on myself. Thanks, Mom.

Contents

Foreword

Kenneth C. DeWitt

I've known Mel Blackwell for over a decade, and from the moment we met, I felt instantly at ease in his presence. Mel has a grounded, attentive way about him. He's the kind of leader who listens deeply and makes you feel like the only person in the room. That's not just a personality trait. It's a leadership superpower.

As a former Integrator in the Entrepreneurial Operating System (EOS) world, Mel lived out what Gino Wickman once said: "The Integrator has the absolute toughest job in the business." Why? Because the Integrator is in the middle, taking fire from both directions. They endure the pressure from a visionary above and the friction of holding a leadership team accountable below. It's not a job for the faint of heart.

Mel not only withstood that pressure, but he thrived in it. He earned trust through calm consistency, made the hard calls with courage, and always stayed anchored to what was best for the business. He navigated tough issues, gave tough love, and led with integrity, all while honoring people. I had a front-row seat to some of those battles and learned a ton walking alongside him.

Mel has the scars, the stories, and most importantly, the insights. He's not speaking from theory. He's speaking from experience. Any room that hears him speak will walk away a little more clear, a little more confident, and a lot more empowered.

Kenneth C. DeWitt, Expert EOS Implementer, Tuscaloosa, Alabama

Introduction

T here's a scene pulled straight out of an old Western that plays out in my mind every time I step into a business that's struggling and riddled with issues that keep it from thriving.

A hot, dry wind sifts grit through the planks of the wooden boardwalk in front of the General Store as the blazing sun beats down on the middle of the street. It's high noon. Movement over by the saloon catches my attention. As a stray tumbleweed rolls lazily down the alley, I can almost hear the iconic whistle that served as theme music in *The Good, the Bad, and the Ugly*. A man in black with a sneer on his face and a six-shooter at his hip straight-arms his way out the doors and struts arrogantly out into the street. Anyone can see that he's looking for trouble.

If he thinks he's going to come into my town to stir things up, he'd be better off to mount up and ride right back where he came from. I straighten my cowboy hat with one hand and step out of the sheriff's office to meet the bandit in the middle of the street.

It's time for a reckoning.

The Wild West of Business

Business truly is like the Wild West. It doesn't matter what a business's website says or how nice their lobby smells. The true test is what's going on behind the scenes. Many days I walk into companies that look like five-star establishments on the outside but are run like a shot-up saloon. Inside everyone's got a gun on their hip and something to prove, but no one's got a plan for what happens after the shootout. In this tough, often chaotic, business environment success seems unpredictable and even unfair. The "bad guys" often win.

But in the middle of the usual slate of characters—the rattlesnakes and the cheats, the poorly trained deputies and the untouchable, mustachioed businessman—there's usually one or two good people. You'll be able to spot them right away. They're the ones just trying to do their jobs while dodging bullets, avoiding scorpions, and praying someone shows up with the guts to lead.

If you're the person with the guts to lead, you need a roadmap that will help keep your business from turning into an all-out stampede the next time things hit the fan. One person can't run an entire business alone. You've got to build a strong internal culture of individual team members who can rise above the inevitable challenges businesses face to become problem *solvers* instead of problem *worshipers*.

But what kinds of problems are we talking about?

Keep One Eye on the Horizon

All is quiet on the home front. Everything seems to be going well. Suddenly you look up and spot a dust trail kicking up in the distance. A gang of outlaws is riding in from the hills. Trouble's coming, and you can't run. That means it's time to get your people in position to defend the town.

Welcome to the wild west of business, where something's always coming for your business whether you can see it on the horizon or not. You can't control what's coming, and you probably won't get a warning shot. By the time you see a challenge, it's already inside the gate. You're constantly fighting against a host of external threats like:

> **Markets:** The domestic or international market can shift like sand under your boots. All it takes is little change in

interest rates, a new trade agreement, a spike in the cost of fuel, or a foreign conflict and your projections are toast. That expansion plan you laid out over bourbon just turned into a cost-cutting conversation over black coffee.

Administration: Washington doesn't know your name, and it doesn't care about your balance sheet. One day the tax code works in your favor, and the next you're paying double to ship a product across state lines. Labor laws change, trade deals get torn up, some senator decides to make your industry the villain of the month. When the administration pulls a lever, your whole market can tilt sideways.

Competition: Business isn't a gentleman's game. You think the folks across town or across the ocean are playing nice? They're not. They're studying your pricing, dissecting your product, and trying to poach your talent while smiling in your face. If they can steal your IP and launch a knockoff before you've had your first cup of coffee, they will.

Customers: Once upon a time, customers were loyal, and brand reputation meant something. Not anymore. One late shipment, bad experience, or slight drop in price from a competitor, and they're gone. You can take it personally, or you can get better. If your customer has to choose between you and someone faster, cheaper, or easier, guess what? They'll choose faster, cheaper, or easier.

Culture: Every generation thinks the next one's soft. That's not new. But what *is* new is how fast expectations are changing. People want flexibility, feedback, mission, purpose, clarity, and accountability all wrapped into one. They want to feel seen and heard without being coddled or lied to. If your leadership model hasn't evolved since the Reagan administration, good luck. You're trying to run a frontier town with a black-and-white sheriff's code, but your team's coming in from a technicolor world. You'd better learn to speak both languages.

Technology: Automation. AI. Cloud platforms. Tech stacks. Chances are whatever you're using now will be outdated by next quarter. If you're still printing reports and walking them down the hall, the gunfight's already over, and you've lost. The fast pace of business is brutal. It takes no prisoners. By the time you finally decide to upgrade, the posse's already two towns ahead, and they're not waiting for you to saddle up.

That's not a short list. You're under pressure for sure, but so is everyone else, including your vendors, partners, customers, and employees. Many businesses are dealing with layoffs, inflation, burnout, shoddy systems, and broken trust every day too. It's bound to spill into your business.

That's not an excuse to lower the bar. That's a reason to raise your leadership and build your business's internal culture so that it's strong, intentional, and impervious to the elements. You lead your people like they're the only cavalry you've got because they are. When the storm hits, the bullets fly, the supply chain breaks, or the customer base dries up, all you'll have left are the people inside your walls and the subculture you've built together.

So yes, keep one eye on the horizon but don't waste your life chasing shadows out there. Build strength from the *inside* so that whatever comes, you're ready. Stop waiting for perfect conditions, hoping the storms will stop. Start building the kind of business that can take a hit, survive the storms when they come, and still move forward, humming with traction and momentum.

The threats outside your gates aren't going away, but you *can* be ready to win.

The Good Guy Can Win

Some folks will tell you the good guy never makes it in business. They'll say the ones who rise to the top are the slick talkers, backroom dealmakers, or those willing to bend the truth or burn a few bridges if it means making their quarterly bonus. If you've spent any time in the wild west of business, I get why you'd believe that. I've seen it too.

Yet the good guy *can* win if they use what I call *uncommon sense*. If you're the good guy, this book will teach you uncommon sense. But who is the good guy in the context of this book? Let's talk about it.

For Good Guys Only

Now, before we go further, let's get something straight. This book isn't just for CEOs sitting in corner offices. It's for anybody who carries responsibility inside a business, whether you run the whole herd or a smaller part of it.

This book is for groups like these:

- **Business owners and entrepreneurs** building something from scratch who need to know how to protect it.
- **Executives and department heads** in established companies who are responsible for a team, a division, or a profit and loss statement.
- **Leaders in mergers and acquisitions,** where two cultures collide and someone has to bring them together as one.
- **Family businesses and succession planning,** where the question is: Who's next in the saddle, and will they be ready to ride?
- **Nonprofits, schools, and even influencers**—because leadership is leadership, no matter the size of your operation. If people are following you, you're on the hook for culture.

This book is also for people who aren't officially "the boss" but who know deep down they've been called to step up. Maybe you're a young leader who doesn't want to learn everything the hard way. Maybe you've been in business for years, but you've hit a wall and can't figure out why the results don't look like they used to. Or maybe you're standing in a season of change. You're selling a business, bringing on partners, or just trying to keep the wagon train moving through a tough stretch.

If any of that sounds like you, you're one of the good guys. And this book is for you.

Uncommon Sense (Where This Book Comes In)

If you've read this far and you're still with me, then you already know this isn't your typical leadership book. There are no trendy buzzwords here. No "synergizing strategic leverage" or "unlocking transformational agility." I'm not trying to sell you a feel-good framework or a four-color quadrant one-sheet with a trademark in the corner.

This book is about cutting through the noise so we can focus on what *actually* works.

Uncommon Sense is a book about the simple, practical, no-fluff wisdom that's so obvious it often gets overlooked but will keep your team together when the roof caves in. In other words, uncommon sense is just common sense that people are too scared, too busy, or too distracted to use.

Inside *Uncommon Sense*, you'll learn the wisdom that comes from staring down the barrel of someone else's gun and living to get the entire wagon train to safety. It's usually the opposite of what you'll hear from consultants who've never struggled to hit payroll or deal with a toxic high-performer.

And before we go any further, let me tell you something I learned after years of fixing broken companies. Most leadership systems leave a gap no one talks about. That includes even the good ones, like the Entrepreneurial Operating System (EOS) outlined in Gino Wickman's book *Traction: Get a Grip on Your Business*.[1]

The way I see it, every organization needs two visions. There's the main vision everyone rallies around. It is the overall direction of the company, and most leadership systems do a good job of determining what the main vision is. They fall

---

[1] Gino Wickman, *Traction: Get a Grip on Your Business* (BenBella Books, 2007).

short when they don't help create the second vision, which I call the *subvision.*

If the vision is the destination, the subvision is the journey. The crazy thing is, while the main vision is unique to each business, the subvision is the same no matter what kind of organization you're running.

Your subvision is to get your people to believe you can all reach the main vision and get them so excited about it that they show up as their best every single day. Without a subvision, they're left wondering, *How are we going to do it? What will it take? Can my leaders get me there? What's in it for me?*

Most companies have never developed a clear subvision. They never discover a way to pass the excitement and determination to keep going all the way from the top of the *org chart* to the bottom. Without it progress will stall out, and your people will give up when things get hard, and it looks like there's no hope.

I wrote this book to be the roadmap that shows you how to

- inspire each individual in your organization to show up as their best self every day,
- carry your organization's vision from the CEO all the way to the ground floor, and
- get people fired up to execute the main vision with excellence.

It will equip anyone in business, from seasoned executives to those just starting out, with the *Uncommon Sense* insights to solve problems effectively, build winning teams, and succeed in the wild west of business.

You don't learn kung fu from the book. You practice kung fu by *using* the book. Along the way, I'll share my favorite *Melisms*—the plainspoken principles I've repeated to every team I've ever led and every leader I've ever mentored.

Here's what you'll learn in each part of the book:

Part 1: The Wild West of Business

What does it mean for a business to truly thrive—not just survive—in today's world? In part 1, I outline the rules of survival in the wild west of business and define what a healthy, high-functioning culture looks like. Through stories of startups, turnarounds, and leadership missteps, you will see how structure, clarity, and cultural alignment are the foundation of a business that wins. In this part of the book, I'll also introduce the *square-wheeled wagon*—one of the biggest problems that keeps businesses from running smoothly. And then I'll show you how to fix things.

Part 2: Creating a Problem-Solving Culture

This section will equip you to shift from a culture of complaining to a culture of action. You'll learn to help your team to stop a practice I call "worshiping problems" so that together, you can start *solving* problems. You'll also learn how to implement effective structure before plugging in people, how to end the chaos of "drive-by meetings," and how to adopt a decisive, gunslinger mindset. These chapters lay the groundwork for building a team that doesn't freeze in the face of challenges—but responds quickly, thoughtfully, and decisively.

Part 3: Creating a Pony-Up Culture

Learn how to foster accountability and role alignment across the business. From the principle that the leader "ponies up first" to understanding when you're asking a "cat to bark," this section shows how to create a culture where every team member takes responsibility for their performance. It also dives into how to identify and remove toxic team members and why trusting people for who they *actually* are—not who you wish they were—is essential to building a team that works.

Part 4: Creating a Powerful Culture

The final section of this book is about embedding excellence and integrity deep into the business's DNA. You will learn how to rally your team around a shared commitment to be their best selves individually and as a team. I'll also show you how to create a safe environment for smart risk-taking ("If you're not wrecking, you're not riding"). You'll also learn why having unwavering principles matters when pressure mounts. The section will end with a direct letter to those starting out in business, offering real-world advice for building a career rooted in grit, clarity, and uncommon sense. The letter will also act as an important reminder to those who have been riding herd and holding down the fort for years.

Plus, interspersed throughout the book you'll find

- real stories from my time in startups and fixups, billion-dollar companies, and smoke-filled trailer park collection rooms (That story's coming up in chapter 2.);
- practical strategies you can start using *today*, not after a three-day retreat or six-month workshop; and

- most importantly, a philosophy of leadership that's built on service, strength, and getting the hard stuff right.

You'll find lessons learned in the trenches and straight-shooting strategies sprinkled throughout the chapters. This isn't dry theory but actionable wisdom based on the direct, hands-on experiences I've seen and felt in startups and fixups.

I've been at this for over 35 years. I've carried the water, swept the floors, managed the chaos, turned around broken teams, and led at the C-suite level for decades. I've seen what happens when leaders hide, and I've seen what happens when they step up.

Trust me, you want to be the leader who steps up. This book will show you how.

Ready to roll up your sleeves, ask the hard questions, fire a few snakes, and build something your team can be proud of? Then saddle up. What's coming next isn't theory. It's a map from a mentor who's helped businesses survive the wild west of business time and time again and lived to tell the tales.

PART 1

The Wild West of Business

Is your organization barely surviving or consistently thriving? In part 1, I'll break down the rules of survival in the wild west of business today. Then I'll show you what thriving looks like so you know what you're gunning for when it comes to having a winning workplace culture.

Chapter 1

The Rules of Survival

On a clear night when there's a full moon—something they called a Comanche moon—Comanche warriors could ride full speed at night. They didn't need lanterns or maps, just instinct, grit, and a skill so sharp it struck fear in settlers who heard the tales and knew they'd never see them coming. As intimidating as it sounds, the warriors knew how to survive in conditions no one else could.

A business won't survive for long operating at full speed by nothing more than moonlight. Yet I see business leaders riding hard in the dark all the time. If you're one of them, you can *trust your gut* and hope it all works out. For a while, it might. You might even convince yourself they're pulling it off. But here's the truth: You're not a Comanche warrior. You can't build a business at full gallop under moonlight and expect to survive for very long.

A thriving business needs daylight. It needs maps, trails, markers, and rules of the trail that everybody follows. It needs people working together toward common goals. Without these basics, you're just another rider flying blind in the dark. Sooner or later you're going to hit a rock or low-hanging branch you never saw coming.

In this chapter, I'll introduce the rules of survival in the wild west of business. Ignore these rules, and your business will fail to survive. Recognize them, and you'll have a fighting chance to move from barely hanging on, to building something strong. But first, let's talk about how to spot the signs of a business headed for eventual disaster.

Is Your Business in Survival Mode?

When you think about the phrase *survival mode* in terms of a business, do you envision a company that's in total chaos and barely keeping its doors open? That's not survival mode. That's a business in crisis, and that alone is a whole separate book. So what *do* I mean when I use the phrase survival mode, really?

A business in survival mode is one that's technically functioning, maybe even producing results, but it's doing so in a way that's unsustainable, exhausting, and broken beneath the surface. Most leaders don't recognize when their businesses are in survival mode. They think their lack of growth is just part of the "grind" or that a new business system will solve the problem.

Yet there are so many businesses out there who have tried systems like Entrepreneurial Operating System (EOS) and are still in survival mode. They go into it thinking that it will be the solution they've been looking for, yet it doesn't seem to stick deep into the business. There's a reason for that. Two reasons, actually.

First, most systems, even really good ones, never make it past the leadership table. They don't cascade down into departments with the same force or clarity. Enthusiasm shrinks the farther the system gets from the boardroom if there's no excitement and buy-in at an individual level. Second, many companies misunderstand the roles of visionary and integrator, resulting in the wrong people trying to do the wrong jobs.

If you know what signs to look for inside your business, you can quickly spot survival mode. There are several signs, and here are the most common ones:

You've tried everything, but nothing sticks.

The bookshelf in your office is full of business books. You've handed them out to your leadership team. You've signed up for webinars, bought personality tests, and jumped on the "flavor of the month" program somebody swore would change your life. And yet here you are, still not getting the results you wanted.

You're getting results, but it's killing you.

You might be hitting the numbers, but it's not sustainable. You're working harder than everyone else around you just to keep the wheels on. Meanwhile, the guy you play golf with seems to have a business that is growing faster and is easier to manage, and you can't figure out why. You can win that way for a while, but it'll burn you out and wreck your home life if you don't change something.

Problems only get pushed up—never down.

If your business is in survival mode, your people are problem finders instead of problem solvers. It's as if every time there's a monkey (or problem) messing up the works, team members walk into your office, drop the monkey on your desk, and walk away. Every issue in the company seems to end up on your shoulders, and you wind up doing other people's jobs instead of your own.

Your culture is fractured.

Maybe you've got cliques or whole departments that cancel each other out. There could be a rattlesnake in the camp—a rogue team member who's building their own little following and undermining your authority. You're exhausted from trying to keep the peace.

There's no unity at the top.

Your leadership team is pulling in different directions. It's like you're all members of the same orchestra, but you're not playing from the same sheet of music. You can recognize the song, but it sounds awful—and you sure wouldn't want anyone else listening in.

Your structure is confusing or nonexistent.

Instead of roles driving the business, you've got people-driven structures that grew out of convenience because you simply plugged in the people you have. You don't even know how your org chart ended up looking the way it does, but you know it's not working.

You can't hold the line outside your walls.

The competition is eating your lunch. New divisions don't take off the way you thought they would, and growth beyond your core market feels shaky.

Your standards are slipping.

You've lowered the bar just to get by. You're keeping poor performers because you can't afford to lose them. You dread the politics inside certain teams or departments, so you avoid dealing with them altogether.

Everyone's burning out.

Nobody takes a real vacation anymore. Or if they do, they're chained to their inbox the whole time. Your people are good, but they're tired, and so are you.

If you recognize yourself in any of these situations, don't panic. You're definitely not alone. These are the vital signs of a business stuck in survival mode. The good news is, there's a way out, and it starts by obeying the three rules of survival.

The Three Rules of Survival

You don't fix survival mode with a new book or a clever hack. You fix it by getting the basics right. Every strong business I've ever built or turned around came back to the following three basic rules. They're simple, but they aren't easy. Ignore them, and you'll stay stuck. Get them right, and you'll finally stop riding full speed in the dark and start operating well because you can see your way forward.

Rule 1: Culture Comes First

Culture eats strategy for breakfast. In my opinion, it always has and always will. Most leaders spend their time kicking up dust about strategy and going all in on meetings with whiteboards and big plans. But if your culture is sick, none of those strategies matter.

But what do I mean when I talk about culture in the world of business? Culture is the ecosystem of your business. Think of your business like an aquarium with culture represented as the water inside the talk. Water conditions determine what can survive inside the tank. Put a freshwater fish in saltwater and it dies, no matter how tough it is. The same is true of your team. If you put the wrong person in the wrong ecosystem, it can kill your business.

Culture is made up of how people interact, what's expected of them, and what kind of behavior gets rewarded or tolerated. Culture also encompasses the hierarchy inside your business such as who you give the badge to. Are the good guys in charge? Or are the culture bandits—team members who question the business's mission and vision—running your town? A culture that rewards hard work, accountability, and problem-solving will thrive. A culture that lets politics, mediocrity, or rattlesnakes take root will rot from the inside out.

Get culture right, and it sustains itself with a little pruning and care. Ignore it, and it'll get cloudy fast like a fish tank you forgot to maintain. We'll talk more about getting the culture right in chapter 3. Now let's look at the next rule.

Rule 2: Build the Right Structure

Once you've set the culture, you need a structure that can hold and help maintain that culture. If culture is the water in your fish tank, structure is the tank itself. It's the necessary frame or container that holds everything together.

Most leaders build their businesses around people instead of roles. That's backwards. When you build your business around a person instead of a role, you end up with a Frankenstein org chart where Bob's in charge because Bob's been here 20 years—even though he's not the right man for the seat. Structure isn't about Bob or Jill or Sam or Margaret. It's about the role. Roles first, people second.

We'll talk more about exactly how to build the role-based structure a strong business needs in chapter 7 so you can start fresh if you need to. But the bottom line is, you can't keep people in a role that doesn't fit them without it affecting the business.

The reason structure is so important is because it drives communication like your arteries drive blood to parts of the body that need it. If communication is clogged or crooked, information never flows right, decisions stall out, and everyone feels like they're flying blind. Get communication right, and suddenly the building stops threatening to topple.

Rule 3: Solve Problems Effectively

Problems need to be solved as close to where they happen as possible. Too many businesses push every issue up the chain until leadership is buried. That bottleneck will crush your leaders and stall your growth.

I learned this young. In my early 30s, I was running a 600-person company full of engineers twice my age. Problems were everywhere, and every one of them ended up on my desk. I decided to make a rule. No one could bring me a problem without a proposed solution. If a person has time to see the problem, he or she has time to think through an answer.

That one rule transformed the business. Meetings stopped being gripe sessions. People started owning their work, thinking like leaders, and fixing issues before they snowballed. And when they did raise an issue, it was paired with a path forward. Not every solution was good, but it didn't matter because the culture shifted. We became a problem-solving machine.

That's what healthy businesses do. They empower people to lead themselves and solve problems at the lowest level possible. Leaders provide support when needed, but they don't carry around problems that don't belong to them. We'll talk more about how to build a problem-solving culture in part two of this book.

Wrapping Up the Rules

Culture. Structure. Problem-solving. You can't shortcut these three rules, and you can't delegate them away. They may not be glamorous concepts, but when you get them right, you'll go from survival mode to building something worth keeping.

The rest of this book will show you how to move from survive mode into thrive mode, but these are the basic nonnegotiables. If you don't get them right, you'll keep riding fast and blind until you hit something that knocks you clean out of the saddle.

From Surviving to Thriving

Now don't mistake me—getting culture, structure, and problem-solving right won't suddenly turn your business into a gold mine overnight. These three rules aren't the finish line. They're just the beginning.

If you've been running flat out and operating in survival mode every day, putting these rules in place in your business gives you the daylight, map, and compass you need to point yourself and your team in the right direction. These rules won't get you all the way to the safety of the fort, but they will keep you from riding in circles or off a cliff so you can make more progress faster.

Once your culture is healthy, your structure is sound, and your people are solving problems instead of handing them off, you're no longer just surviving. You've laid the foundation to start thriving. That's when business starts to feel different—lighter, more sustainable, and even enjoyable again.

In the next chapter, we'll talk about what thriving really looks like, and how to build best practices that create growth rather than burnout for yourself or your people. Before anything else, take a breath. Survival mode is no place to build a future. You've got to step out of the shadows of the Comanche moon and start leading in the daylight.

Chapter 2

Thriving in the Wild West

Would you believe me if I told you I started my professional career in a trailer park? Right out of high school, I took a job as a collector at a mobile home financing company. My first day on the job, I walked into the office through a cloud of cigarette smoke—everyone smoked on the job back then—to see everyone just sitting around.

I was young, excited, and ready to get to work. They must have seen how eager I was, because they didn't waste any time handing me the worst portfolio in the place—the one with all the accounts nobody else wanted—and told me, "Good luck." I'm sure they didn't think I'd last a week, and I might not have if not for Tina.

Tina was my mentor, and she was tough as nails. Now that I think about it, she was a lot like Miss Kitty on *Gunsmoke*— strong with a good head on her shoulders and a soft spot for underdogs. She must have seen something in me, because she took me under her wing and made sure I learned how to do my job right. To my credit, I listened to everything she said. I wanted to know exactly what to do, when to do it, and how.

Everything she told me, I did, right down to the last detail. She had the kung fu, so I didn't improvise or try to be clever. I just followed the playbook she created for me, and I worked my tail off.

And you know what? It succeeded!

Right out of the gate, I hit my daily, weekly, and monthly quotas. It wasn't long before I was the top collector in the region. How? I was barely even old enough to vote, and it wasn't that I was smarter or more charming than my coworkers. The reason I succeeded at an unusual level was because I used Tina's advice to guide me, and I worked harder than most.

That job was my first exposure to the power of a mentor and a model (or proven process to follow). I've been a big believer in mentorship and following what works ever since.

A Mentor and a Model

My first real job lit a fire in me to learn more, and I decided to go to college to study business leadership. I took every leadership role I could get my hands on, graduated with two degrees, and went seeking my next mentor and model.

After graduation, I was offered one of the biggest opportunities of my career—a greenfield market launch for USA Mobile out of Knoxville, Tennessee. This was a totally new market for the company. At the age of 25, I became the sales manager for East Tennessee. Mark Roth was my boss's boss and mentor, and right away, he told me something I'll never forget.

"Your job is to download the DNA of this company and make it walk around on two legs inside other locations."

It was a tall order, but I took everything my mentors told me as gospel. And that's what I did. Again they had the kung fu, and I followed it to the letter. I internalized the DNA of USA Mobile—learned all the systems and processes and dialed in on what made things tick. Then I went to work "installing" it into a brand-new location by hiring and training the new team.

I didn't hire flashy salespeople. I hired mature people who already knew how to lead, even if they didn't have direct industry experience. What was the result? That location had the #1 most successful launch in the history of USA Mobile, which grew to become a $100 million company while I was still working with them. They were then acquired by Arch Wireless.

Nobody expected my team to succeed because I was so young and the team was brand new. We outperformed everyone because every day, each individual showed up as their best self. We worked together in teams as our best selves, and we never missed a single quota ever. Every single person on that team eventually went on to lead their own business.

My leadership wasn't always so well-received though. After Knoxville, I was sent to Montgomery, Alabama to take over a failing USA Mobile location. And when I say failing, I mean the business was completely overwhelmed to the point it was underperforming. Even the sign on the front of the building said "USA Mob" because the "-ile" was burned out.

It was a mess. Nobody was hitting their quotas, and the place was located in an area that was well-known for being a drug den. The only thing I inherited when it came to my team was low morale and bad habits. It took everything I had to turn that business around.

At first, I held onto a few people I shouldn't have. I tried to make things work and gave some of them too many second chances. That slowed down the turnaround some, but eventually, I made the tough calls that needed to be made. Within a month, we never missed a single quota again. Within a quarter, the Montgomery store was performing as well as any other store in the company. I still succeeded, but it was a harder, longer fight.

These two experiences taught me a lesson I've carried into every business since:

Culture isn't a side effect—it's the *whole* game. If you build a strong culture, your team will pull in the same direction, solve problems where they happen, and protect each other like family. Get it wrong, and no strategy in the world will save you. I've seen billion-dollar companies crumble because they let a rattlesnake sleep in the crib with their baby, so to speak. I've also seen scrappy startups dominate because their culture was tight as barbed wire.

Good business culture isn't inherited. It's built one decision at a time. Some team members saw the vision, or shared direction and goals, and followed. Others didn't, and they didn't stay employed. I stayed consistent, coachable, and tough. These fledgling businesses and acquisitions thrived.

That was just the beginning. Over the last 35 years, I've led in startups, turnarounds, and billion-dollar companies. I've held VP-level C-suite titles for more than 20 years. But it's not the title that holds the power. The title gives you the perspective you need to apply learned wisdom and execute on proven best practices every day.

Plain and simple, I figured out what worked and did it over and over again. I learned how to get best practice to filter down from the CEO to the janitor. That's what made me successful. And now, these methods are what I teach.

Even all these years later, I still quote Tina, and I still hear Mark's voice in my head. But these days, I'm the mentor. I speak, coach, and consult with leaders who want their teams to run stronger and faster—with more alignment. But before I talk about *how* to thrive in the wild west of business, let's first define *what* a thriving business looks like.

Signs of a Thriving Business

A thriving company doesn't mean everyone's riding unicorns to work and singing kumbaya around the break room coffee pot. Thriving in the wild west of business is about having a team of employees who are pulling everything inside the business in the same direction and operating with balance and clarity.

In a thriving company, the culture is genuinely good. It's supportive, not toxic. You walk into the office (or log into the Zoom room) and you can feel it. The team functions like a well-oiled machine. People know their jobs and do them to the best of their abilities. Each person is in the right seat, playing to their strengths instead of being forced into roles that make as much sense as asking a cat to bark.

And because the right people are in the right places, you don't have culture bandits running around stealing morale.

If they pop up, they're dealt with quickly and firmly, because protecting the culture isn't optional. It's part of everyday survival for a business leader.

What's one of the biggest tells that a business is truly thriving? People actually take their vacations. Not those fake "I'll still check email three times a day" vacations, but real ones where people feel like they can be off the grid, guilt-free—if they want to be. When systems and coverage are solid, folks can step away without fear the wagon train (AKA your business's progress from where you are now to where you want to go) is going to fall apart.

A thriving business will set vacation coverage on the calendar and celebrate when people unplug. Your team members will come back rested, grateful, and (often) so moved they'll give you a hug with tears in their eyes when they come back to work.

So how do you get to that point? Everything in this book is based on five simple best practices that are simple, proven ways of doing business that actually hold up when the dust storm hits. When you put these five best practices into action, you can build an organization that doesn't just survive the wild west of business, but actually thrives in it.

Five Best Practices to Thrive

Thriving in business requires a different approach. You need a set of practical, battle-tested best practices that incorporate the right underlying philosophies. Remember how I said good guys absolutely *can win* in the introduction? They can. The key to thriving in the wild west of business is wrapped up in five best practices:

1. Getting rid of the bad guys
2. Serving the good guys well
3. Doing a little bit more
4. Practicing the Hedgehog Effect
5. Creating vision and shared language

Let's take a closer look at each one.

Best Practice 1: Get the Bad Guys Out

Here's the truth nobody wants to say out loud—some people don't belong in your business. When you have a team member who's pulling against you, not with you, that's a sure sign they're on the other side of the rope in the tug-of-war contest. People who want to pull from the other side of the rope are culture bandits, and they shouldn't be on your team.

Culture bandits might look good from the outside. They nod in meetings and smile in the hallway. They might even outperform a little here and there to stay under the radar. But beneath the surface, they're rattlesnakes sowing distrust, poisoning morale, and draining the life out of your culture.

Even worse, culture bandits never leave on their own. They need the job. So if you don't remove them early, they'll stay just long enough to infect the people you *do* want to keep. By the time you notice the damage, it's already too deep to deal with easily.

That's why the first part of leadership is protection. You protect the mission, the team, and the culture. Do it fast, do it early, and don't apologize for it. Now that doesn't mean you lead with fear, rule with an iron fist, or fire first and ask questions later. Protecting the mission, team, and culture means you're crystal clear about what matters, and you consistently defend those things that matter most. We'll talk more about removing culture bandits in chapter 3, but for now, let's get into serving the good guys.

Best Practice 2: Serve the Good Guys Well

The second part of leadership is serving the good guys. The ones who are on *your* side of the tug-of-war rope. Identify the good team members and lift them up. Reward them when they perform well. Make sure they know you see them. Make them feel special.

What leadership *really* looks like.

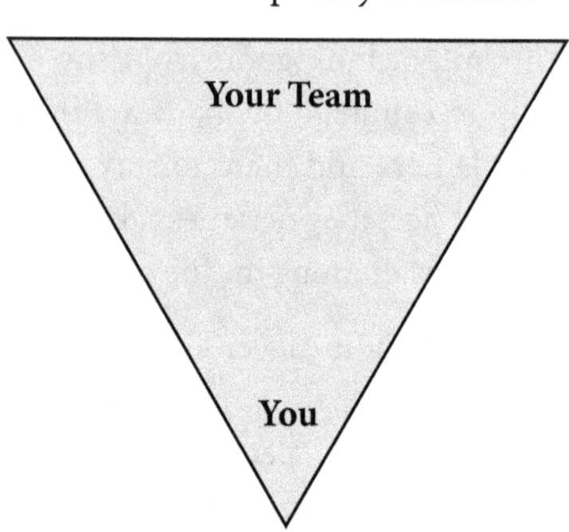

Think of leadership like an inverted triangle. Your name is at the *bottom* of that thing, not the top. You're holding up the team—not sitting on their shoulders. You're not here to be served. You're here to serve the ones who show up, buy in, and do the work. And the truth of the matter is, you can't lead a great team if you're too busy protecting the wrong people.

Get the bad guys out so you can serve the good ones like they're your cavalry. Then watch what happens.

Your team will start to trust you.

Your culture will get lighter, sharper, and faster.

Your good people will stick around longer and bring their friends.

Deep down everybody wants to be on a team that wins. People want to be their best selves when they see that modeled by their leader. They will walk through the desert for a leader who tells the truth and does what's right. Being that kind of leader is hard.

Being a good leader is always hard. But if you procrastinate on fixing issues or outsource all the hard stuff, all you're doing is dragging out the pain over time. Don't be willing to let the good people suffer while you delay doing what needs to be done.

And don't wait around for a perfect team, either. Perfect doesn't exist. Aim for finding the right people and putting them in the right roles. When you do that, you can lead a group of flawed human beings to outperform someone else's team of flawed human beings by doing just a little bit more. And that's where we're headed next.

Best Practice 3: Do a Little Bit More

Most people think that to win in business, you have to finish the horse race 12 lengths ahead of the competition. They try to blow the doors off the competition by outspending, outhiring, and outmarketing the competition. But that's not how things work. More often than not, you win by a thread.

If you want to win in the wild west of business, what you really need is to do a *little bit more*.

- Create a *little bit more* clarity in the morning huddle.
- Have a *little bit more* follow-through on tough conversations.
- Be a *little bit more* disciplined in your hiring process.
- Institute a *little bit more* accountability when things start slipping.

Why does doing a little bit more work? In business, the margins of victory are razor-thin. If your team outperforms the competition even by a little bit, you win. What separates the teams that hold together from the ones that fall apart isn't a 10X miracle. It's a 1% edge that compounds over time. Want me to shoot straight? In all honesty, your team doesn't have to be perfect. They just have to be a little less dysfunctional than the one across the street.

I've seen it play out again and again. The other guys had bigger budgets, fancier buildings, and flashier org charts. They were able to outspend us, outmarket us, etc. *But* we beat them because we were a little more aligned. A little more focused. A little more consistent. And each person showed up as their best self a little bit more often.

And they never saw us coming. By the time they realized we were a threat, we'd already passed them.

Most teams can't hold things together for long and will crumble under pressure. If your team works together even *a little bit* better than theirs, you win.

The trick of it is you have to be consistent. You don't do a little bit more for a week and call it a culture. You do that little bit more every day. You build a team that refuses to settle and then you lead with urgency, precision, and a relentless desire to improve.

If you keep this up, one day soon, you'll look up and realize you're not behind anymore. You're ahead.

Best Practice 4: The Hedgehog Effect

Have you ever seen how a hedgehog acts when it's threatened? It doesn't run, and it doesn't fight. It curls into a ball with its spines facing out. That's it. The hedgehog digs in and focuses on the one thing it does better than anything else: survive.

I call this the Hedgehog Effect. It's super simple, and it really works. Apply this concept to your business and you'll have one of the most powerful advantages a business can have—excellence. Here's how to put the Hedgehog Effect to work in your business:

Step 1: Focus on one area where you want your business to be world-class.

Step 2: Become the best at that one thing and continue to pursue excellence relentlessly every single day.

That's it. In the wild west of business, distraction is everywhere—new tools, new trends, and new tactics. Everybody wants to chase shiny objects. But when you're trying to win, chasing everything is how you lose.

I've seen companies flame out because they tried to be all things to all people. But I've never seen one fail because they were too good at what mattered most to their business goals and vision.

So ask yourself, what *one thing* can your team do better than anybody else in your space? What's the thing you want to win at? It might be operational speed. Or customer service. It might be low-cost execution, innovation, or relationship management.

Whatever your one thing is, commit to it and go full hedgehog. Every decision from that point forward gets filtered through that one thing.

- If it strengthens your one thing, you do it.
- If it weakens your one thing, you don't.

The Hedgehog Effect works because most of your competitors are scattered and reactive. They're trying to do too much, please too many people, and keep too many plates spinning. And while they're distracted, you're digging in.

Leaders who win aren't doing 50 things halfway. They're doing a few things with relentless focus. And speaking of focus, the final best practice that will help you win in the wild west of business is something really important. Turn your attention toward vision and shared language.

Best Practice 5: Creating Vision and Shared Language

I was 18 years old the first time I saw Art Williams speak. He is the founder of A.L. Williams, a multibillion-dollar network marketing company and one of the most successful insurance companies in American history. I was a whippersnapper really, still green to the world of business. But the memory feels like it was only yesterday because it had such a profound impact on my life.

It was 1987, and I was sitting in a regional A.L. Williams' office in Montgomery, Alabama watching a closed-circuit satellite broadcast. Then this guy showed up on the screen. It was Art himself, and he started pacing around on camera like a man on fire, talking about what it takes to win in business. I'm sitting there, fresh out of high school, not even out in the real world yet. But I felt something shift.

Williams wasn't talking about spreadsheets or credentials or pedigrees as markers of business leadership success. He was talking about internal fire and mental toughness. That's what successful leadership looks like.

> People in America won't follow or believe in a negative, dull, disillusioned, frustrated, dad gum cry baby. People want people that are positive and excited and enthusiastic and tough.[2]

---

[2] Arthur L. Williams Jr., *Just Do It*, video recording, 1987, uploaded by Primerica Leader, April 14, 2011, 45:32, https://www.youtube.com/watch?v=Y3yWjjJ2jI8.

I never forgot that. And as I watched him lead tens of thousands of people through a screen, it clicked for me. People don't follow titles. They follow the person who is confident in the mission they're pursuing and can clearly communicate their vision.

And if I could operate with that same kind of clarity, belief, and vision, I could win too. So I copied and pasted that right into my brain and let it come out through my actions and communication style.

For the last 35 years, people have told me I have "Pied Piper energy." At first, I thought it was a part of my personality—some sort of gift. But the longer I've been operating out here in the wild west of business, the more I realize that creating and communicating a vision and shared language isn't something only a few people can do. It's not a personality trait that you either have or don't have. It's a best practice. It can be defined, taught, and executed with excellence.

But what do I mean by vision and shared language?

> **Vision** is what unifies the team. Everyone should have a clear understanding of where you're going as a business.

> **Shared language** is all the stuff you say and do to carry that vision out. It's also the related tools you use to communicate about what needs to happen. Meetings, dashboards, reports, email, documentation, technology, and everyday conversations are all part of a business's shared language.

When you have a vision and shared language, you're effectively getting everyone's horses pointing in the same direction *before* you use your spurs. It doesn't do much good to yell, "Go faster!" if nobody knows which direction to go, right?

A good vision and shared language creates alignment so strong that the bad guys practically out themselves because they just plain can't fake having a good vision and shared language for long. It becomes obvious who doesn't belong in the business's culture. Bad-fit team members can't execute on a vision or speak a language they don't understand.

I've used this best practice in every turnaround I've ever led from Knoxville to Montgomery and to billion-dollar enterprises. I've walked into total chaos, and the first thing I do before firing anyone or rebuilding any structure is to start uniting the language and clarifying the vision for an organization.

Nothing works if people aren't on the same page. No amazing strategy. Nothing.

People will follow clarity and energy. Not confusion and complaints. Art Williams taught me that too. And I've seen it play out a thousand times. If you want to build a team that follows through when it gets hard, you've got to give them something worth following. But don't worry—you don't have to be a born speaker or a motivational guru to do this. You just have to believe deeply, communicate clearly, and repeat the vision relentlessly.

Vision and shared language is how you move a business from reactive to resilient. It's also how you build trust fast. It's also how you make sure that when the dust kicks up and the shootin' starts, your team's riding the same direction instead of off on six different trails. Shared vision is one of the most important prerequisites for getting the culture right, which we'll talk more about in chapter 3.

I know these best practices aren't flashy. Practicing them won't get you a TED Talk. They work every single time, yet most people overlook them because they're chasing complexity. They think the answer has to be the latest tech or the most complicated strategy: big, new, or branded. The real answer usually lies within these five best practices and using what's simple and right in front of you as leverage.

Leverage is Power

As I wrap up this chapter, I want to talk about something really important that doesn't get the attention it deserves—leverage. Leverage, sometimes called traction, makes it possible to accomplish more with less. If there's one thing I've learned in my years building teams, turning around broken businesses, and leading from the front, it's that hard work alone won't get you to where you want to go. You need leverage.

Don't get me wrong. I believe in working hard, and I've out-hustled a lot of people over the years. But if all you've got is hustle with no leverage, you'll burn out before you break through.

Part of thriving in the wild west of business is knowing where the leverage is and *using* it.

When I launched that Greenfield market for USA Mobile in Knoxville, I didn't have a single lead or reputation to lean on. I had to build it all from scratch, including the entire team. But we never missed a daily, weekly, or monthly quota. How?

We used leverage. And here is a list of the different types of leverage that can be used and how I used them in Knoxville.

Boss leverage: Learn from good leadership, then take action on it. In USA Mobile, I had a leader who gave me a clear vision and a proven playbook. I didn't question it. I took action, followed the playbook, and it worked!

Staff leverage: Hire the right people and train them well. I hired mature people who knew how to lead, not just sell pagers. I gave them standards, not slogans, and they rose to the occasion.

System leverage: Create systems that *work*, then operate them and optimize as you go. We met every morning and every evening. We fixed every square wheel the moment we saw it. If something didn't work, we either made it work or got rid of it.

Self-leverage: When you're put in charge, take charge. I didn't wait on motivation. I led *myself* first in my position with USA Mobile. I became an example for my team because you can't scale chaos—not in others and not in yourself. I knew that if I wanted to lead people better that I needed to start by leading *myself*.

Culture leverage: Set clear expectations to encourage and incentivise team members to follow them. Our expectations at USA Mobile were so clear and so high that the team held the line even when I wasn't in the room.

That team became the most successful new location in the history of the company because we knew how to leverage what we had. Even in Montgomery, where I took over a store on its last legs, the same rules applied. Once I stopped making excuses for the underperformers and cleaned house, we turned things around in a month. And like I said, within a quarter, it was one of the top-performing locations in the region.

That wasn't luck. That was leverage.

But not all forms of leverage are created equal. You don't beat dysfunction with hope alone. You beat it with structure, clarity, and discipline. You beat it by building a team that's more aligned, more accountable, and a bit more dialed in than the one across town.

The greatest leverage you'll ever have is your business's *culture*.

Your business's culture is the silent engine under everything. If it's broken, nothing works. If it's healthy, everything gets easier. So in chapter 3, we're going to start where every strong business starts—inside. It's time to talk about building a culture that can ride out the storm when things go sideways on the frontier.

Getting the Culture Right

After 35 years in business, I can tell you with 100% certainty that culture eats strategy for breakfast. The idea of culture eating strategy for breakfast certainly isn't new. It's a phrase you may have heard before. Nobody seems to know who said it first, but it's a statement I'd be willing to die on a hill for. You can spend months polishing a perfect strategy, but if your culture is sick, that strategy is dead on arrival.

Culture isn't optional. It's not a side dish you get around to after the "real business" of strategy and numbers. Culture *is* the business. But that doesn't mean getting it right is easy.

Have you ever thought to yourself, *My company would be great if it weren't for all the people in it?* I ask that question in a tongue-in-cheek way, but think about it. Companies are made up of people, and people are dysfunctional. By default then, dysfunctional people introduce dysfunction into companies. You can't avoid dysfunction, but you can fight like hell to minimize it and maximize effectiveness.

And the strongest weapon you can wield against dysfunction is a strong culture.

That's why culture has to come *before* strategy. Get the culture wrong, and all your plans, organizational charts, and shiny PowerPoints won't mean a thing. Get the culture right, and your people will all be working together toward the same goal regardless of inevitable bumps in the road.

In this chapter, we're going to talk all about getting the culture in your business right. Because if the culture isn't right, even the best strategy in the world won't save your business when challenges arise. Let's start by talking about what you must do if you really want to get your company's culture right.

Set One Vision Shared by All

The first thing you must do to get the culture right is set a shared vision that you have already made sure is shared by all.

History gives us a striking example of how powerful a shared vision is from the Bible. It's a familiar one you've probably heard in Sunday school or church: the Tower of Babel. The story goes that the people of Babylon were completely united. They spoke the same language, believed in the same purpose, and decided to build a tower so tall it would reach the heavens.

According to the story, God looked down and saw what they were doing. "Look!" God said. "The people are united, and they all speak the same language. After this, nothing they set out to do will be impossible for them!"[3] A group of flawed human

____

[3] *The Holy Bible*, New Living Translation, (Tyndale House Publishers, Inc., 1996, 2004, 2015). Scripture quotations used by permission.

beings were unstoppable simply because they were aligned in vision and language. The only way to slow them down was for God to scatter them by confusing their language so they spoke multiple languages. Once they couldn't communicate, the vision for the tower fell apart.

Now whether you take that story as scripture, myth, or a leadership parable, the takeaway is clear—when people share one vision and one language, there's no telling what they can accomplish. Think about that. The combination of a united people who all speak the same language is supernatural. It is more than a dialect. It is an effective two-way communication.

That's what culture with alignment looks like. It's why a business with the same resources as its competitors but with a unified vision can lap the competition in results. They may both serve the same market, pull from the same talent pool, and

use the same tools. But if one company is united in vision and execution, and the other isn't, the united organization will come out ahead every time.

A company divided by unaligned culture is just Babel all over again. Everybody's building, but nothing gets finished. People spend more time arguing about the blueprint than laying bricks. Before you know it, projects stall out, and the business starts to falter. But when the vision is clear, when the leader gets everyone speaking the same language, you don't just have a company. You've got momentum that feels unstoppable.

Picture an orchestra. In an orchestra, you have dozens of musicians, each with their own instrument, their own part to play, and their own ego. Left to themselves, instead of music, you would hear chaos. But when the maestro steps up and gets everyone playing the same sheet of music, the mess turns into a symphony. That's strong culture.

Will things in your business be perfect with a strong culture? No. Conflict will always exist because we humans are messy. You'll always have someone who wants to bang the cymbals louder and somebody else who thinks you need more cowbell. But unity isn't about everyone having to like every decision. If the vision is clear, and the leader is strong enough to get everyone playing in harmony, the little imperfections won't derail the mission.

Now let's take a look at some examples of the difference having a strong culture can make. Here are some stories from businesses I've worked with that reveal how powerful a strong culture is for a business.

Case Study 1: Cracking the Code with a German Company
One of the best lessons I ever learned about culture and shared vision didn't come from an American company. It came from a German multinational that handled exhibit and trade show setups for companies like Volvo.

In Germany, they had it nailed down. They were dominant in their market, highly respected, and their way of doing things had worked beautifully on their home turf for the past 40 years. But when the American subsidiary tried to copy and paste the German playbook, it fell flat and wasn't doing as well. What made the brand special from a European standpoint was missing, and nobody on the American team could see that. After 20 years of coasting along, the American brand of the business had stagnated. It wasn't broken, but it sure wasn't thriving.

That's where I came in. We tore down their entire approach to marketing and positioning in America and rebuilt it from the ground up while still honoring the European best practices. Instead of part numbers and engineering-heavy messaging, we retooled the story for how Americans buy. We changed who the organization targeted, how they spoke to that audience, and how the product was positioned. Almost overnight, the results shifted. That American subsidiary went from flatlining to dominating their market.

Here's the part I'll never forget: The Germans were watching. Instead of dismissing what we'd done, they flew me over to see their operation firsthand. I walked their halls, studied their systems, and then showed them how we had adapted their model to fit a different culture. They not only respected what we had done, they paid attention and started implementing a few things they'd learned from us about culture, copying and pasting them across the German markets.

That was a huge compliment. And it taught me something important: Shared vision doesn't mean one-size-fits-all. The Germans had the vision, but they needed someone who understood the American market to adapt it without losing their core DNA. It took mutual respect—me respecting their heritage and systems, and them respecting my experience and willingness to retrofit what they had. That mutual respect is what made buy-in possible for their business on both sides of the Atlantic.

We accomplished all of this through collaboration and working together. And once the Germans and the Americans were pulling in the same direction, that company dominated its hedgehog everywhere they operated.

One vision shared by all isn't optional. Once the direction in a business is set, everybody needs to walk out with the same message working towards the same goal. If even one person decides to go rogue on their own and take a few people with them, you've got a coup brewing. And that will undermine a business faster than anything else. That's why the next thing you must do to get the culture right is remove culture bandits.

Remove Culture Bandits

I'll never forget the time I told one simple story and completely split the room.

I was standing in front of a few hundred senior leaders from a multibillion-dollar privately held enterprise. Presidents, vice presidents, general managers—the whole brass. The CEO had brought me in as a hired gun to help fix a dozen of their underperforming businesses. Nobody really knew me yet, but they all knew why I was there: Something wasn't working and leadership wanted answers.

So I told them about a rattlesnake in a baby crib.

The story was simple: If you've got a rattlesnake curled up in your baby's crib, it doesn't matter how pretty it looks or how much you think you need it, you don't let it stay there. You get the shovel, chop its head off, and toss it in the parking lot. Period.

The reaction was instant. Half the room went stone-faced, looking horrified—like I had just slapped their mama. The other half laughed out loud, nodding in total agreement. And right there, at that moment, I knew exactly who would deal with a rattlesnake problem if they had one and who wouldn't.

A hand shot up: "But what if that rattlesnake is really important to the business?"

My answer was the same: "Then it's even *more* important that you get rid of them."

That sent another ripple through the room. More horrified faces. More nervous laughter. And then the next question came: "Why wouldn't you try to work with them? See if they'll come around?"

That's when I told the old Russian fable about the scorpion and the frog. The scorpion convinces the frog to carry him across the river, promising not to sting him. Halfway across, he stings the frog anyway, dooming them both. The frog gasped, "Why did you do that?"

The scorpion replies, "Because it's my nature."

And that's the point. Just like a rattlesnake will always be a rattlesnake, a culture bandit will always be a culture bandit. It's their nature.

That 30-minute discussion hijacked the entire agenda. The room was split between the leaders who knew they had a rattlesnake problem and were relieved someone finally called it out, and the leaders who were terrified because they had built their businesses around one. Either way, the truth landed hard: If you tolerate a rattlesnake in your business's culture, you're putting the baby at risk.

I talked briefly about getting the bad guys out in chapter 2. "Bad guys" is another word for culture bandits. If it helps, you can think of company culture like a watering hole that serves a herd of cattle out on the range. Just like a healthy watering hole contributes to a healthy herd of cattle, a healthy culture helps maintain a healthy, thriving team. If you've got a culture bandit poisoning the watering hole, even the strongest in the herd will be affected.

Once you set the cultural direction, everybody's got to be on board. If you're sitting at the leadership table when the vision gets set, you've got the right to argue and wrestle—and even bloody up your elbows. But once that direction's decided, you're either pulling the rope with the team or you're out. There's no middle ground. Having a culture bandit at the top is one of the fastest ways to sink a business. You can't let a snake stay in the crib, no matter how talented or how valuable they seem.

The Problem With Culture Bandits

Culture bandits are talented, often charismatic people, who decide the rules don't apply to them. They nod in the leadership meeting, then walk out and whisper a different story to their teams. They're smart, they're persuasive, and they're dangerous because they create a counterculture that pulls people in another direction.

Have you ever tried to row a boat with somebody paddling the opposite way? That's what it feels like to lead a business with a culture bandit. So much energy gets wasted trying to keep things straight.

Left alone, culture bandits gather a following. They unite behind their own version of the truth, their own vision, and their own language. Before you know it, you've got a Tower of Babel inside your company. That's not only counterproductive; it's sabotage.

This is where leaders often hesitate. They think, *But I can't afford to lose her; she knows everything about our systems* or *he brings in too much revenue to risk letting him go.* But here's the reality: If someone is poisoning the culture, they're already costing you more than they're worth. You're protecting a rattlesnake because you're afraid of the bite, but every day you leave it in the crib, the risk of a more serious consequence grows.

And let's be clear—it always starts at the top. The most dangerous rattlesnake isn't the low-level employee with a bad attitude. It's the VP who undermines decisions, the manager who badmouths leadership to the team, or the cofounder who's half in and half out. When the poison comes from the top, it spreads twice as fast and does twice the damage.

There's only one solution: You get the shovel. You cut the head off and drag it out of the crib. And you do it quickly, because hesitation here is what kills companies.

I've seen too many leaders protect culture bandits because they were scared of the fallout, scared of retaliation, or scared of being left without a replacement. But the truth is, you can't build a thriving culture on fear. You build it on courage. And nothing says courage louder than protecting the team by removing the one person everybody knows is a problem, and nobody is willing to confront.

That's leadership.

Case Study 2: The Culture Bandit in Pensacola

Let me give you a real-world example of how some uncommon sense helped me deal with a culture bandit.

I once had a market manager down in Pensacola. He was a young guy I had promoted out of sales. He was a great salesperson, sharp as a tack, but green as grass when it came to managing people. He opened a new branch and hired a team. On paper, it all looked fine. But one of those hires turned out to be a rattlesnake.

This rattlesnake was talented—no question. He was dynamic and domineering. And he took over that branch like it was his own personal fiefdom. Within months, other good employees were threatening to quit because they couldn't work with him. The market manager kept calling me, saying, "I don't know what to do with this guy."

"Have you fired him yet?" I asked.

"I've never fired anyone before."

That's when I realized that I had promoted a top salesman into management without teaching him how to wield the shovel. That was on me, and it was up to me to fix it.

So I drove down there myself. We held the meetings, gathered the facts, and it was clear as day. This guy had to go. But when the moment came, my market manager and even my boss, a man in his 60s, tried to talk me out of it. "It's almost Christmas, Mel…maybe give him another chance."

Nope. Not happening. Not with a rattlesnake in the crib.

I looked that employee in the eye and said, "You've tried harder to get fired than anyone I've ever seen. You've disrupted the team, poisoned the culture, and there's no way you didn't know this was coming. You're done." We gave him severance and benefits for 45 days—plenty of runway to land somewhere else—but he was out.

Here's what happened next: The branch's sales picked up almost immediately. The turnover stopped. The team stabilized. In other words, the culture was saved practically the minute the rattlesnake was gone.

But something unexpected happened a year later. I got a Christmas card from that very same guy! He thanked me and said he'd cleaned up his life, started going back to church, and that his family was happier than ever. You read that right: He actually *thanked* me for firing him.

That's the power of protecting culture. Firing someone isn't easy. But sometimes the most merciful thing you can do—for the company and for the individual—is to grab the shovel, throw the culture bandit out, and save the baby.

Clearing out the culture bandits is only half the job though. Once the crib is safe, you've got to take a hard look at who's left and where they're sitting. Because here's the truth: Even good people can sink a business if they're in the wrong role. It's not always about bad actors—sometimes it's just misalignment. A culture bandit poisons the well on purpose, while a misplaced person poisons it by accident. Either way, the result is the same: frustration, wasted energy, and a team that feels like it's rowing with a huge hole in the middle of the paddle. That's why after you protect the culture, the very next move is making sure the right people are in the right seats

Put the Right People in the Right Seats

At first glance, this responsibility seems easy. Of course you'll put the right people in the right seats. What you may not realize is it's very easy to get this one wrong. You want to hang on to good people, so you put them in a role that's available. But there's a problem with that.

Just because a role is available doesn't mean it's the *right* role for the person you're putting into it. When you put the right person in the wrong role, it's like entering your best mule in a horse race, and then getting mad when it doesn't win. Is it a great mule? Of course. But it doesn't belong in a horse race. In fact, you're selling it short of its potential by forcing it to perform in a role it's ill-suited for.

Imagine dropping a cactus in the Arctic Circle. You can do it if you want, but it's not going to grow. The same goes with people. If you drop the wrong person into the wrong culture, they'll wither. Worse yet, sometimes they'll start poisoning everyone else. Then you're dealing with a rattler in the crib, and we all know how that's going to go.

I call this type of management asking a cat to bark. A cat is not a bad animal. In fact, cats are great at being cats. But what they're not great at is being dogs. When you ask a cat to bark, it's going to fail miserably. Even worse, it's going to *be* miserable and so will everyone else around them because everybody knows cats aren't meant to bark.

The truth is, somebody out there is praying for that role you're trying to fill. They're wired for it, gifted for it, and chomping at the bit to get in. But you'll never find them if you keep trying to squeeze the right person into the wrong spot. Plus it's not fair to your good players. Nothing drags down a high-performing team faster than forcing them to drag along someone who's misplaced. The rest of the crew knows when a seat's filled wrong. They see it. They cover for it. And they resent leadership for ignoring it.

We'll talk more about teaching a cat to bark in chapter 11, but for now if you realize you've got a cat sitting in a dog's chair, don't waste six months waiting for a meow to turn into a bark. Fix that misplaced role now.

Getting the right people in the right seats will steady the wagon, but it won't guarantee smooth travel. Even when you've set a clear vision, gotten rid of the culture bandits, and stopped asking cats to bark, there's still one more outlaw that can derail the culture: the bad habit of worshiping problems instead of solving them.

Break the Habit of Problem Worship

I've seen it a hundred times. Whole teams will gather around, wring their hands, and pass the same problem around like it's the town idol. They dissect it, analyze it, and complain about it—but nobody ever actually solves it. That's problem worship. And in the wild west of business, problem worship will get you killed faster than a well that goes dry in the middle of the summer.

Tell-tale signs of problem worship show up when problems get pushed up the chain instead of solved where they occur. Suddenly meetings are full of "grave concerns" but light on action, and people get rewarded for explaining the problem eloquently instead of fixing it.

That's so backwards! In a thriving culture, problems don't get worshiped, they get tied up and thrown down like a wild steer that's always breaking fences. We'll talk more about worshiping the problem and how to create a problem-solving culture in part 2 of this book. But first, let's take a look at how a big transformation can occur when a company leaves problem-worshiping behind.

Case Study 3: Killing Problem Worship in a Software Startup

A few years back, I stepped into a healthcare software company that was circling the drain. It was during the Obamacare era, and on paper they had everything—a sharp CTO writing the code, a visionary founder, a director of operations who knew her stuff, a small sales team, and a support staff. When you walked into the office, it was set up professionally with nice furniture. Yet they'd invested millions already and were burning cash fast, closing almost no business.

The culture was pure problem worship. The sales team would "try" calls, then pass every warm lead to the founder because *he* was the only one who could close. They had no scripts, no quotas, and no accountability. Meetings were just gripe sessions—everybody explaining why things weren't working instead of working to actively fix anything.

So I went straight to work. We set up sales boards, made daily activity goals, created scripts, and had morning huddles and evening reviews every day. We also added energy and excitement with bells on desks so every closed deal got celebrated. In 30 days, momentum shifted.

By 90 days, the company was hitting targets it had never touched before. The meetings stopped circling the same drain. Energy spiked and results skyrocketed.

That company went from the edge of collapse to consistent, sustainable performance. There was no magic wand, but when I showed them how to stop worshiping the problem and start solving it, everything changed.

When you stop worshiping problems and start solving them, you create momentum. People stop feeling like victims and start acting like owners. When a whole team thinks that way, they move faster than the competition. Because while everyone else is still staring at the problem, your team's already riding off with the solution.

Signs of Success

So how do you know when you've actually got the culture right? What does it look like in the wild where the dust is flying and the work is real? Here are the signs:

People are happy to contribute. Not just punching the clock, but showing up ready to add value. They want to be part of the mission, not just part of the payroll.

The team feels balanced. Folks know their roles, and the workload doesn't crush them. They've got room to breathe, think, and do their best work.

They know how to contribute effectively. The vision is clear, the language is shared, and people don't waste time second-guessing what matters.

People are in the right seats. No cats are being asked to bark. No mules are strapped into racehorse saddles. Everybody's playing to their strengths.

Culture bandits are absent—or dealt with fast. If someone tries to poison the well, the team knows leadership will handle it. That builds trust.

You'll also notice the ripple effects. Conflict doesn't disappear, but it gets managed. Dysfunction doesn't vanish, but it doesn't consume the place either. Folks go home at the end of the day not only less exhausted, but better. Better dads, better moms, better coaches, and better friends. They're not dragging workplace poison back to the dinner table; they're bringing home the version of themselves they're proud of.

That's the mark of a thriving culture. People want to stay, they want to contribute, and they want to get better—not only for the business but for themselves.

Getting the culture right isn't a one-time roundup. It's the steady work of setting the vision, guarding the camp from rattlesnakes, and making sure every rider is in the right saddle. Do that, and the outfit doesn't just hold together—it starts to move with real force. Folks know where the wagon train's headed, they trust the systems, and they can ride hard without burning out. That's when you know you've built a camp worth belonging to.

But culture doesn't police itself. Somebody has to set the tone, defend it, and keep the fire burning. And that job always falls on the leader. Which brings us to the next big question: are you cut out to lead?

Chapter 4

Are You Cut Out for the Job?

I'll never forget the time the chief technical officer of a business I'd been hired to help tried to hold the whole company hostage.

This guy was no slouch. He was an Ivy League graduate and a brilliant coder. He'd written every line of the software that powered the entire business, which was based on this software. On paper, he was gold. In practice, he was toxic. At every meeting, he dragged the team back into excuses. At every accountability step, he pushed back. He had all the classic culture bandit behaviors dressed up as "helpful feedback."

I finally pulled him aside.

"Look, I've been watching you," I said to him as he sat on the other side of my desk. "Every time we set direction, you drag the conversation back to problems. Every time the team makes progress, you throw water on the fire. You're a smart guy, no doubt. But you're not aligned, and you're not going to change.

That makes you the problem. And I don't allow problem worshippers in this company."

I thought that was a good, strong warning. But turns out it hadn't made a lick of difference. It wasn't long before he crossed the line. He walked into my office one day, leaned back in his chair, and essentially picked up the baby—the business—and put a gun to its head.

"I'm taking my family on vacation," he said, "and when I get back next week, I'll decide whether or not you get to keep the code."

I had been really nice to him up to that point, and he had really underestimated me. I wasn't ready to tip my hand just yet though. I stared at him without flinching for a long moment, then I spoke.

"Wait a minute now. What is it that you are asking for?" Nobody takes a business "baby" hostage like that without asking for something, and he was no exception.

He smirked, figuring he had me cornered. After all, without the code, we didn't have a business. So he named his price. He wanted a rather hefty percentage of equity and a big, fat salary. Why not shoot for the moon? After all, I couldn't very well say no, could I?

He didn't know what *I* knew though. And that's once a rattlesnake bares his fangs like he was doing, you don't negotiate. You grab the shovel.

"Are you sure you want to do this?" I asked calmly, looking him square in the eye. "You've put me in a really bad spot."

With his chest puffed up, he pushed himself out of his chair and strode over to the door of the office. At the last second, he turned around and said over his shoulder, "I'll be back in a week."

"Alright," I said as I watched him go.

When he walked back into my office a week later, I didn't hesitate. The moment I saw him, I said, "You're fired. Get your stuff and get out."

"What?" His face went from smug to stunned in an instant. "You can't fire me. You need me. This company will fall apart without me. I'm looking out for the good of the company."

"No, you're not," I said. "What you're doing is slowing us down, poisoning the culture, and keeping this team from winning. I cannot believe you picked this baby up, put a gun to its head in front of me, and thought that I was going to do anything but shoot your ass. I said you're fired, so get your stuff and get out of here!"

We lawyered up, made sure the code stayed with the company, and cut him loose that same day. The difference inside the company was immediate. It was like everyone on the team released the breath they'd been holding. The weight lifted. Now we could really start to win.

That moment birthed one of my core principles of leadership: Never put down your gun if you're the last good guy in the room. When you're the one responsible for protecting the culture, the baby, the business—you don't blink, and you don't back down.

And that's what this chapter is all about. Leadership in the wild west of business isn't for the faint of heart. It will test you, stretch you, and sometimes scare the hell out of you. Are you cut out for the job?

Leadership isn't about titles. It's about being the one willing to do what the situation requires, whether that means standing steely-eyed like Clint Eastwood when a rattlesnake threatens the baby or walking back into the corral like a shepherd to tend the wounded.

Are you willing to be that person? Before you decide, let's take a look at the qualities an excellent leader should possess. At the end of this chapter you'll have a chance to do a self-assessment to gauge where you are and where you might need to start shoring up your skill sets.

Essential Qualities of a True Leader

So how do you know if you're cut out for the job? It isn't about IQ, Ivy League degrees, or your slick LinkedIn profile. Leadership comes down to traits that show up when the bullets start flying and the stakes are high. Some of these you may already have, and some you'll have to cultivate. But if you're not willing to chase after them, you're not ready for leadership in business. We'll go deeper into some of these characteristics later in this book, but here are the essentials:

> **Tough but fair**—You'll run into rotten eggs and rattlesnakes. A real leader deals with them head-on. He or she is firm but not petty, and decisive but not cruel.

Decisive—There will be times as a leader that you'll need to gather what you need to make a smart call, then make it. Don't get stuck in analysis paralysis while the wagon train stalls and the water rises.

Fearless of failure—Innovation requires risk. If you're not wrecking, you're not riding. Fail fast, fix fast, move forward.

Chivalrous—Leadership is about respect, especially for those with less power. Be tough with your peers, but humble enough to take off your hat and listen to those who depend on you.

Cultivator—Like a farmer, your job is to create an environment where your people can grow and thrive. If the crops aren't producing, check the soil before you blame the seed.

Discerning—Don't fall for the myth of the "Superman employee," as if the world sits on the shoulders of one person and will fall apart without them. Build systems that work *without* depending on one person holding all the cards.

Objective—You can't lead well if your emotions call the shots. Sometimes you have to step back, strip away the drama, and do what's best for the business, even if it's not your gut instinct response.

Humble—Be willing to learn from your team, from the front lines, and from your competitors. Pride kills as many companies as bad strategy does.

Straightforward—People need clarity. Speak plainly, even when the truth is hard to hear. Fluffy words make for fuzzy execution, and confusion never helps anybody.

Willing to do tough things—Leaders step into the fire when no one else will. If a heavy load needs to be carried, it's the leader who will shoulder the burden.

Responsive—Leadership isn't stubbornly clinging to your plan. It's listening, adjusting, and responding to what the business and your people need.

Punctual—If you can't respect time, you can't expect respect. Set the tone by showing up when you say you will.

Creative with purpose—Invite ideas and innovation, but know when to stop brainstorming and make the call. Creativity without closure is chaos.

Focused and able to prioritize—At the end of the day, your job is to strip away dysfunction and get the orchestra playing the same song.

Don't panic if you're not perfect in all these qualities. Nobody is. You just have to be willing to get better. We all start somewhere. Do this quick self-assessment to gauge your starting point so you can give yourself credit where credit is due and highlight areas for improvement. Be honest. Where are you strong? Where are you weak? This isn't about beating yourself up; it's about knowing what you're working with and where you need to grow.

Essential Qualities Self-Assessment

Rank yourself on a scale of 1–5 on how well you feel you embody each characteristic, with 1 being "poor" and 5 being "excellent." It can also be helpful to have someone close to you fill it out with you in mind, as it can be hard to be objective about our own qualities.

Tough but fair

1   2   3   4   5

Decisive

1   2   3   4   5

Fearless of failure

1   2   3   4   5

Chivalrous

1   2   3   4   5

Cultivator

1   2   3   4   5

Discerning

1   2   3   4   5

Objective

1   2   3   4   5

Humble

1   2   3   4   5

Straightforward

1   2   3   4   5

Willing to do tough things

1   2   3   4   5

Responsive

1   2   3   4   5

Punctual

1   2   3   4   5

Creative with purpose

1   2   3   4   5

Focused and able to prioritize

1   2   3   4   5

Living up to all these qualities of leadership may seem daunting, but remember—you don't have to do it all alone. As a leader part of your responsibilities is to know when it's time to delegate and elevate, and then do it.

Delegate and Elevate

You don't have to be world-class at every single one of the qualities of leadership. Work toward becoming better than mediocre across the board, then lean hard into your strengths and build a team to cover your weaknesses.

The principle of *delegate and elevate* comes from inside the Entrepreneurial Operating System (EOS) Gino Wickman teaches in his book, *Traction: Get a Grip on Your Business*.[4] Most leaders nod their heads at the idea of delegation but very few actually practice it well.

Here's how it works:

First, elevate yourself in the areas you're strong. If you're naturally skilled at something like decisiveness, creativity, cultivating people, for example, then lean into it. Make it your lane, and elevate yourself in it.

Then delegate responsibilities you're weak in to someone who's strong in that area. Don't ignore your weak areas. You can't fake it forever. Find someone you trust who reports to you and delegate that function intentionally to a person who can carry it.

This is where humility comes in. A lot of leaders think admitting weakness makes them look soft. Wrong. Pretending you don't have weaknesses is what kills you. A strong leader says, "I'm not great at this, but I'm going to find someone who is—and together we'll win."

---

[4] Wickman, *Traction*, 130.

Think of it like a cattle drive. You might be the best at reading the trail but not the best at keeping the herd watered. That's fine. Elevate yourself to trail boss, but make sure you've got a trusted hand managing the water. If you try to do both, you'll burn out and lose the herd.

On the other hand make sure you're truly delegating and elevating, *not* delegating and levitating. Delegate and levitate happens when a leader refuses to fully hand off tasks. Instead they hover in the background, meddling in an assignment that isn't theirs. It's a funny mental picture, but it will bring progress to a halt inside your business.

Need another example of delegate and elevate? Think of the orchestra example I introduced in chapter 2 where I compared strong culture to an orchestra that makes beautiful music together. Well leadership is like conducting an orchestra. The maestro doesn't pick up every instrument and try to play it himself. He doesn't grab the violin from one hand and the trumpet from another. His job is to know enough about each section—the strings, the brass, the percussion—to bring them together on the same sheet of music.

That's what delegation and elevation look like in real life. You don't have to be the best at everything in your business. In fact, you can't be. What you *do* have to be is the one who sets the tempo, unites the players, and makes sure everyone is moving in harmony toward the same end.

If you're not a strong communicator, you'd better find someone who is a pied piper and can carry the tune for you. Because without clarity, the orchestra doesn't make music. It makes noise.

At the end of the day, leadership isn't about playing every part perfectly. Leadership is about creating the conditions where everyone plays their part so well together that the result is bigger, richer, and more powerful than anything one person could produce alone.

The best leaders I've seen not only know their strengths; they know their limits. And they build teams that plug those gaps. Instead of wasting time asking cats to bark, they find the right dog for the right job and get out of the way.

Delegate what you can't do well. Elevate what you can. That's how you stop being a bottleneck and start being a true leader.

Pale Rider and the Shepherd

I don't want to leave you with the idea that leadership is easy. It's not. A leader carries a burden the rest of the team doesn't have to. You're the one who has to step forward when everyone else would rather stay behind.

Sometimes leadership means being the Pale Rider.

If you've ever seen Clint Eastwood in the 1985 movie *Pale Rider*, you know what I'm talking about. He plays a mysterious preacher who rides into a mining town that's being bullied and squeezed by a greedy land baron. Nobody else has the courage to stand up to the oppression, but the preacher does. He doesn't raise his voice, he doesn't strut around; he quietly straps on his gun belt and walks out into the street. Calm. Steady. Deadly serious. And when it's time to do the hard thing, he does it.

That's what leadership looks like sometimes—being willing to step up and confront what nobody else has the stomach for. Putting down the bully. Taking out the rattlesnake. Protecting the town, your people, even when it makes you the target.

Other times, leadership means being the Shepherd.

That's the part the movie doesn't show, but it's just as important in business. A shepherd watches the flock, makes sure the weak don't get trampled, listens for the ones who are hurting, and pulls strays back into the fold. Every person on your team is walking around with an invisible sign on their chest that says, "Make me feel special." A good leader sees that and responds to it.

True leadership means carrying both roles. Sometimes you're the Pale Rider—the steely-eyed protector, willing to do what no one else will do. Other times you're the Shepherd—the patient, steady guide who helps people grow and heal.

To be honest, neither role is entirely comfortable. Both take courage. Both take humility. And both are required if you're going to survive in the business. And speaking of survival, we've talked about what thriving looks like. But anyone who's been in business knows that sometimes it's a challenge to just *survive*. The truth is, there are certain rules to survival in the wild west of business. And in the next chapter, I'm going to give them to you.

The Square-Wheeled Wagon

I once walked into a telecom company that swore they had a sales problem. "Our salespeople just aren't producing," they told me. "If we could get them to work harder, we'd be fine."

But when I looked closer, I realized the problem wasn't the horses. It was the wagon.

Picture a team of good horses hitched to a wagon with square wheels. It doesn't matter how strong or determined the horses are. When the wagon has square wheels, they're going to struggle. They might lurch forward for a while, but sooner or later the axle breaks, a wheel falls off, or they wear out. Momentum is impossible when the wagon is broken.

This is what I call the square-wheeled wagon problem, and that's exactly what was happening in this company. Leadership kept blaming revenue, when the real issue was systemic. The customer experience was terrible, the compensation plan was confusing, and the product delivery was unreliable. They weren't asking their people to sell software; they were asking them to sell a lie. No wonder the "horses" couldn't pull it.

Leaders sometimes misdiagnose their issues, chasing surface symptoms like revenue or effort, when the true drag is deeper—buried in their structure, culture, or processes. And until you fix the wheels, no amount of whipping the horses will make that wagon roll any smoother.

In this chapter, we're going to dig into what square wheels—faulty systems—look like in a business. There are three vital signs that throw up red flags when you have a systems problem: revenue, cost, and profit. I'll show you how to identify the red flags in each vital sign so you know where to put your attention first. If you want lasting momentum, you can't just hire stronger horses. You've got to smooth out all the square edges on the wheels of the wagon they pull so your business can roll smoothly along, gaining speed as it grows.

Revenue Problems: Square Wheels Kill Momentum

Revenue is the first place most leaders point the finger at when the numbers don't look good. When revenue dips, the cry goes out, "We need more sales!" More sales can fix any issue, right? Wrong. More revenue can fix *some* problems, but more often than not, the real issue lies deeper.

To identify whether your revenue vital signs are blinking yellow or red, track the momentum of your revenue. Healthy systems produce a steady amount of revenue, month after month. If you have a systems problem, you'll notice inconsistent revenue that appears in bursts and stalls. Imagine a square-wheeled wagon that lurches forward with a sharp burst of strength from the horses, then comes to a halt again almost immediately. The stop-and-start progress not only kills your numbers, it wrecks your reputation in the marketplace. Customers can sense when you're running ragged.

If you're seeing inconsistent revenue, look for the following red flags. That's where you're experiencing a systems breakdown.

Bad Customer Experience

Your sales people promise the world, but when customers walk through the door, they don't get what they were sold. Poor customer service and poor interactions with frontline employees affects future sales and makes existing customers less likely to buy again or refer others to your products or services. If you have a customer service problem, you'll see it manifest in your company reviews, and the average lifecycle of a client or customer will be short. After all, who wants to stay with a company that has poor customer service?

Bogged Down Sales Processes

Do your sales processes and compensation structure keep your sales team bogged down in paperwork or jumping through hoops to make commission? Every hour your sales team spends digging through red tape or fighting your compensation plan is an hour they aren't selling. This self-inflicted "sales tax" is a momentum killer and a heavy price to pay.

Broken Product Delivery

You can't expect a salesperson to close deals if the product shows up late, wrong, or in pieces. Reliability matters. When you ship weeks later than promised—or worse, with quality issues—you're forcing your sales team to drag that square-wheeled wagon uphill while apologizing to customers the whole way.

Think of it this way: Every sales organization starts back at zero on the first of the month. The sales quota resets to nothing, and the climb begins again. If the wagon wheels are square, the climb feels like running on a treadmill set to max incline. The slope becomes unbearable after a time, and eventually your best people will burn out. Make no mistake about it. If your product delivery system is faulty, your sales team isn't quitting because they're bad at selling. They're quitting because they're tired of being forced to pull an impossible load.

Revenue problems are rarely about salespeople not working hard enough. They're about leaders making decisions that build unnecessary drag. If you don't fix those square wheels, you'll keep asking your people to do the impossible, and sooner or later, they'll stop trying. But revenue issues aren't the only indication that you have a systems problem. Let's talk about the next red flag area that indicates systems issues—cost problems.

Cost Problems: Bought Right Is Half-Sold

The next area of business that often throws up red flags for faulty systems is costs. Have you ever heard the phrase, "Bought right is half-sold"? If you negotiate well and control your costs on the front end, you've already won half the battle. Every dollar you save when you buy is a dollar you don't have to make up later in sales.

On the flip side, every dollar you overspend is another notch of slope on that treadmill your sales team will have to climb. If you're careless with costs—signing bloated contracts, failing to negotiate, or letting expenses run wild—you're making it harder and harder for the wagon to move, no matter how good your horses are.

I saw this up close and personal when I worked with a company in the global exhibit and events industry. This company created trade show booths—and I'm not talking about your neighborhood lemonade-stand-sized booths—no sir! These trade show booths were two-story structures sometimes thousands of square feet in size. They were built with custom carpentry, electrical, graphics, the works. The cost buckets, or separate expense categories, were enormous in this industry.

They included not only the physical booth costs, but sales time, travel time, industrial design, fabrication, and trucking.

In this particular company, nobody was owning these cost buckets. No one was taking responsibility for the different expense areas and ensuring they were getting the best quotes and prices. They were operating with one big, mysterious pool of expenses.

One of the first things I did in that company was assign ownership. Every project had someone responsible for each major cost bucket. They all reported to a project manager, who worked with me to make sure costs were driven down without sacrificing quality. That's right. You don't have to cheapen the product to drive costs down. In this company, the quality stayed the same, maybe even got better. But our costs dropped like a rock because people finally took ownership and did the work to get the best price.

As I worked with them, they became one of the highest-priced providers in the market, yet still remained one of the most profitable. Why? Because while everyone else was slashing quality to save a buck, we were driving costs down while protecting quality. Having a low-cost operation with high-quality products really is a sweet spot and a great goal to strive for.

But let me make one thing clear: Cost discipline doesn't mean you have to insist everyone descend into penny-pinching nonsense. I call that type of behavior toilet paper management. In other words, don't save a nickel by replacing Charmin with sandpaper in the bathrooms. That's not leadership; that's insanity. Tripping over pennies while dollars are rolling out the back door will not help your company thrive.

The goal is to keep costs honest and efficient, not to starve your business. Manage your costs well and help your team embrace the *bought right is half-sold* mindset so your wagon can roll smoother and faster without wearing the horses out.

Now let's address the third area that can throw up red flags if you have systems issues: profit.

Profit Problems: Paying People to Pull the Wrong Way

The third vital sign is profit. Seems simple: revenue minus costs equals profit. But I've seen more businesses trip over this one than you'd believe. It's not because they can't do math, but because they're paying people to pull the wagon in the wrong direction and they don't even *realize* it. If you have issues in your compensation systems, the square wheels will become obvious rather quickly. Here are some common complaints you'll start to hear:

"Our reps don't care about profitability."

I've walked into companies where sales leaders said those exact words to me. In reply, my first question is always the same.

"Do you *pay* them on profitability?"

They usually look at me like a cow chewing its cud. Blank stare, no answer. If you reward sales reps for closing deals no matter the margin, they'll happily sell unprofitable deals all day long. Why wouldn't they? They get their commission, and you eat the loss.

The fix for this is simple. Build profitability into the compensation plan. For example, if a rep sells at 95–100% of the target margin, their commission rate stays the same. But if they dip below 95%, their commission decelerates—say, 2% less than standard. You're not rewriting the entire plan, you're putting a disincentive in place for bad deals.

And if your people won't accept that? You've got the wrong people. If your reps are making big money while you're losing money, that's not sales. That's sabotage. Align the pay with the profit, and you'll be amazed at how fast behavior changes.

"Our customer service team is running off our customers."
There's another common complaint I've heard a lot. My return question to that statement is always, "Do you incentivize your people to keep customers happy?"

Nine times out of ten, the answer is no.

Again, people do what you pay them to do. If a customer service representative's paycheck looks the same whether they delight a customer or tick them off, why should they go the extra mile?

The fix is straightforward: Tie part of their compensation to customer care. It doesn't have to be complicated—link bonuses to satisfaction scores, retention rates, or simple follow-up surveys. Make sure the message is clear that team members get rewarded for leaving the customer better off than they found them.

If you don't pay for it, you can't expect it. Align the incentives, and suddenly customer service stops being a revolving door and starts being a reason people stay.

But listen, sales and customer service teams aren't the only places where profit problems show up. Let's take a look at one more area that may need to be addressed:

Executive Pay and Misaligned Priorities

One of the most shocking places I see square wheels is at the top of the org chart. I've sat across from executive VPs of sales, directors, and even C-suite leaders whose compensation wasn't tied to profitability or customer satisfaction. Instead, they were paid strictly on revenue growth.

Think about that. You're paying senior leaders to chase top-line numbers, even if it means slashing margins, burning out customers, or leaving a trail of wreckage along the trail for the rest of the company to clean up. And then you wonder why profits lag or customer churn is through the roof.

To fix this you must add the right factors to the compensation plan. Maybe it's a profitability target, a customer satisfaction score, or both. You can institute bonuses for hitting the marks or penalties for falling short. Either way, you're telling your executives: "We don't just want sales, we want *sustainable* sales that protect the brand."

When you structure compensation in this way, you change the conversation at the leadership table. Suddenly the question is no longer "How much did we sell?" It's "Did we sell it profitably?

Did we deliver it well enough to keep the customer?" That shift alone can smooth out a lot of square wheels.

The truth is, if your executives are making big money while the business is bleeding, that's not leadership. That's malpractice.

Product Delivery, Operations, and Internal Alignment

The same principle applies deeper in the business, especially on the product delivery and operations side. Whether it's manufacturing, logistics, or implementation, product delivery and operations teams have enormous influence over customer satisfaction. And they impact both external customers and internal ones, like sales and service.

I've seen plenty of companies where departments are at war with each other—not in a sheriff vs. outlaw kind of way, but their incentives are misaligned. Operations might cut corners to hit output targets while customer service takes the heat for the fallout. Sales might hand off messy deals and disappear, leaving delivery scrambling to clean it up.

If your departments are creating problems for each other with no incentive or disincentive to fix that behavior, then you've got a compensation problem, not only a culture problem.

Need an example? Let's say your sales team tends to check out after the deal closes, even though part of their role is to stay engaged and ensure the customer's success. They've already collected all their money at the time of sale. There's no reason for them to care what happens next.

To fix this, build engagement incentives into their compensation plan. Tie a bonus or penalty to customer retention or post-sale satisfaction. Hold a portion of their commission until after the first renewal or delivery milestone. Whenever you can, keep your teams financially (and emotionally) invested in the customer's success.

You can do the same thing with collections. If sales or service has any influence over keeping customers current, tie a small piece of compensation or recognition to timely payments. Reward the behaviors that reduce friction and improve cash flow.

And remember, incentives don't always have to be financial. Recognition programs, quarterly contests, and interdepartmental awards can create healthy competition and unity at the same time. Sometimes a simple public acknowledgment or team contest can drive as much engagement as a cash bonus.

The real goal is to look at every team and ask, "What's the ideal behavior?" Then make sure you're rewarding that behavior while discouraging the behaviors that drag the wagon backward. Whether it's through pay, recognition, or shared goals, alignment beats friction every time.

Smoothing Square Wheels in Profit Systems

You've probably figured out by now that one of the quickest ways to spot a square-wheeled wagon is to trace the money. Look at where incentives are misaligned. If you're rewarding behaviors you don't actually want, you're only making your wheel more square.

Now here's where it gets interesting—so pay attention. When you try to fix compensation plans in systems that are broken, you'll often get pushback. Salespeople will say, "I can't be paid on profitability; it's not my fault the company is so inefficient." And you know what? Sometimes they're right. That pushback is gold. It shows you exactly where the wagon is broken. If your people refuse to be tied to a result because the system itself is flawed, they've pointed you straight to the square wheel you need to fix.

I learned this lesson from my old professor, Dr. Petty, who taught me that money can only ever be neutral. Too much or too little both cause problems. In business, the best you can do is align pay so people are pulling on the same rope, toward the same vision. When you get that right, comp plans stop being a source of drag and start becoming a tool for traction.

But if you don't? You're paying people to fight against you. There's no horse on earth strong enough to pull a wagon when half the team is straining against the harness.

Escaping the Comfortably Miserable State

When faulty systems exist in your business, you'll often see a certain condition start to creep in. I've seen this condition in a lot of businesses, and I call it being *comfortably miserable*. Nobody wants to be labeled that, but once you hear it, you know exactly what I mean.

Comfortably miserable looks like this: People complain about how hard things are, how broken the systems feel, and how heavy the wagon is. But they never actually change anything.

Why? Because they'd rather live with the devil they know than face the discomfort of change. The pain of the status quo feels safer than the unknown pain of fixing it.

I've seen entire teams stuck here. They've been burned by too many false starts like flavor-of-the-month leadership programs, new books, personality tests, or some boss's "big idea" that fizzled out in six weeks. After enough broken promises, trust erodes. So when a leader finally comes along with a real solution, people cross their arms and think, *Sure, I've heard that before.*

I get it. Change *is* hard. Swapping out square wheels for round ones takes work. It creates friction. It makes people nervous. But staying comfortably miserable is worse. Comfortable misery drags everyone down, and not only the strong ones who can grit their way through. Business is a team sport. It doesn't matter if one or two horses can handle the load. If the rest are dying in the harness, the wagon still isn't going anywhere.

That's where your leadership comes in. It's your job to define the bridge between the old way and the new one. Show your people that new systems are safer and better, and then walk them across it. Don't throw a bag over their heads and drag them kicking and screaming—that only breeds fear. Instead, lead by example, invite them across, and when they get to the other side, they'll thank you.

But here's the catch: That change has to start at the top. Too many leaders think comfortably miserable only applies to their employees. Wrong. The change has to start with you. If you're the most powerful person in the business, ask yourself honestly: *Am I willing to change for the better?* Because if you aren't, nobody else will.

Fixing the Wheels

Faulty systems (square-wheeled wagons) are some of the most common traps I see in business. Good people (your best horses) are straining against a load that no one could reasonably pull. Leadership keeps blaming effort, sales, or revenue when the real problem is deeper. Broken customer experience, bloated costs, and misaligned compensation plans (that reward negative behavior) only exacerbate the problem. Square wheel after square wheel keeps your wagon stuck.

And then, instead of fixing the wagon, too many businesses settle into being comfortably miserable. They complain and struggle, but they don't change. They'd rather put up with the grind they know than cross the bridge into the unknown.

That's not leadership. Leadership means identifying the square wheels for what they are, calling them out, and having the guts to change them. When you do this, you're lowering the slope of the treadmill and giving your team a smoother path.

Change isn't easy. But if you've read this far, you already know staying stuck is harder. The next part of this book is going to show you how to make those changes. We'll explore how to build a culture and a structure where problems get solved instead of handed up, where the wagon runs smooth, and where your people can finally stop pulling a square-wheeled wagon with no end in sight.

You don't need stronger horses. You need rounder wheels.

PART 2

Creating a Problem-Solving Culture

You've read all the business books and launched all the initiatives, yet still your team members aren't meeting their goals. Diagnosis? You may have a culture of problem-worshiping. In part 2, you're going to learn exactly how to get your people to stop worshiping problems and start *solving* them. We'll also cover how to build structure first, eliminate drive-by meetings, and lead with a clear, decisive mindset.

Are You Worshiping the Problem?

I magine a dusty frontier town that's been harassed by a down and dirty outlaw for weeks. Every evening, the townsfolk circle up outside the general store to talk about their problem. But instead of making a plan and taking action to fight the marauder who's been ravaging their town, they stand around staring at his wanted poster. They point out how mean he looks, how high the bounty is, and how dangerous he must be. But nobody saddles up to actually go after him.

It sounds ridiculous, doesn't it? Why don't they do something? Surely you or I would never sit back and let problems fester… would we?

Think about your last company meeting. Most meetings start with everyone gathered around the boardroom table with a big cup of coffee and end with a long list of problems nobody is prepared to deal with. The discussion of one problem leads to another. The longer the meeting goes, the longer the list grows.

When the meeting ends, the team walks out feeling like it was a productive meeting because ten problems were identified and handed off. They mentally dust their hands off and think to themselves, *Wow I feel so much better! I'm glad somebody's going to take care of those problems!*

Except nobody does. Instead of feeling like something has been accomplished, leadership walks out feeling like they're carrying a half-dozen monkeys on their backs. How are they going to find time to deal with all these problems? How can they do their own job and everyone else's too?

When team members start treating the discovery of a problem as the finish line instead of the starting line, they're worshiping the problem. That's not good, because admiring, dissecting, and making sure the boss knows about the problem isn't the same as taking responsibility for fixing it. If you build a culture that worships the problem, your business is dead in the water. Leadership will get overwhelmed, the front lines will stop thinking, and the whole organization will stall out waiting for someone else to do their job.

So the first question I want you to ask yourself is simple: Do you have a culture of problem solving or a culture of problem worship? One will grow your company, and the other will choke it to death. Let's talk about the signs of a problem-worshiping culture so you can determine if this is an issue you're facing.

What Problem Worship Looks Like

I can spot a problem-worship culture a mile away. Meetings sound like therapy sessions where everybody unloads about what's broken, what's frustrating, and what's in the way. People feel like they've done their job by naming the issue, when in reality, all they've done is toss a monkey on someone else's back.

Why do I keep talking about people carrying monkeys around on their backs? Back in the 1970s, *Harvard Business Review* published a classic article called "Management Time: Who's Got the Monkey?"[5] It's been quoted for decades because it nails one of the biggest traps leaders fall into. It states that every time an employee brings you a problem without a solution, they're really handing you a monkey. And if you take it, that monkey climbs up on your back. By the end of the day, you've got a whole troop of them riding around, and you're stuck feeding and caring for issues that never should've been yours in the first place.[5]

That's exactly what happens in a problem-worship culture. People treat problems like a game of hot potato instead of owning them or putting them where they belong. The higher up you go in the company, the more monkeys you collect, until your executives are suffocating under a pile of other people's work. It's no wonder they can't get traction. Instead of thinking at the level they're paid to, they're spending their energy babysitting monkeys.

Here's the truth: We don't do other people's jobs. We do our own jobs.

When leaders start doing their team's work, who's doing the leader's job? Nobody.

That's how you end up with weak suction—leaders pulled down into the mud or patching fences instead of protecting the fort. Every time you ride out to fix a problem that belongs to someone else, you leave your leadership post unguarded.

The walls weaken, the gates sag, and pretty soon everyone's scrambling just to keep the outlaws out.

It might feel noble to think, *I'm helping my team.* But it's actually dangerous. Covering for subordinates who won't take ownership doesn't make you a hero. It makes you a hostage. You can't steer the wagon train if you're constantly jumping off your horse to walk someone else's. Every time you pick up

---

[5] William Oncken Jr. and Donald L. Wass, "Management Time: Who's Got the Monkey?" *Harvard Business Review*, November–December 1974, reprint 99609.

someone else's monkey, you leave your own horse untied—and the whole operation slows to a crawl. That's how mediocrity sneaks in: not with one big failure, but with a thousand tiny moments of misplaced effort.

And the crazy thing is, some folks are fine with it. They'd rather stay comfortably miserable. They complain about problems, point them out in meetings, and even feel important for doing it. But when it comes down to taking action, they have no interest in solving the issues. For them, the misery of the status quo feels safer than the discomfort of change. If you don't break the habit of worshiping problems, you end up with leaders buried in monkeys and employees who'd rather wallow in misery than grow.

I've seen leadership teams choke under the weight of all those monkeys. Every conversation becomes "Hey did you get me my solution yet?" Nothing moves forward because the people at the top can't possibly carry every burden in the business. And they *shouldn't*. The best person to solve most problems is almost always the one closest to it—the one who actually feels the pain.

But you have to be careful about how you present that to your team. When they come to you with a problem, and you suddenly flip the script on them and say, "Nope. Sorry. Solve it yourself," it's not going to go over very well. The first step to moving your company from problem worship to problem solving is to sell them on the reason why solving their own problems is the best thing for the company *and* for them.

The Reason: Problem-Solving Creates Growth

When I was a kid, I wanted nothing more than to keep up with my older brother and his buddies. They were four years ahead of me, stronger, faster, and always headed off into the woods on their bikes. I'd tag along as far as I could until my bike chain fell off. Every time it did, I was stuck. I couldn't fix it, so either my brother had to circle back and rescue me, or my dad had to come put the chain back on. And once that happened, my ride was over.

Tired of always having to come to my rescue, my older brother eventually showed me how to put my own bike chain back on. The first time I did it myself, I felt like I'd won the lottery. Suddenly, I could keep going. I could ride into the woods with the big dogs. Of course, that meant I got lost a few times, but isn't that what happens? When you solve one problem, you open the door to bigger problems. That's just how growth works—new level, new devil.

It's the same in business. If your people can't "put their own bike chains back on," they'll never run with the big dogs. They'll keep stalling out, waiting for somebody else to come save them. This makes the whole team and the whole business suffer. Once people learn to handle their own problems, they grow the skills that prove they're ready for the bigger challenges that come with real growth. I always make sure to tell the teams I work with something like this:

"I'm not punishing you, but if you want to run with me—if you want to run with the big dogs—then welcome to the new world. You've got to solve problems. The good news is, I'll teach you how."

Teaching your team to solve their own problems helps them put themselves back on their own bikes so they can ride further. Because the truth is, you're not paying people to point out what's broken. You're paying them to think, to solve problems, and to grow. Once they understand *why* it's important for them to take ownership of the problem in their areas, give them a rule for *how* to do it.

The Rule: Do Not Present a Problem Without a Solution

Do you want problems to get solved? Of course, but you shouldn't have to be the only one solving them. To get everyone in a problem-solving state of mind, instate one simple rule:

No one is allowed to bring a problem to the table without at least one possible solution attached.

Does the solution have to be perfect? No. It doesn't even have to be the solution you end up using. But if someone has time to notice a problem, they have time to think about how they'd fix it.

This simple rule changes everything. Meetings stop being gripe sessions and start being work sessions. Instead of weighing leadership down with monkeys, the team member keeps the monkey on their own shoulder and shows up with an idea for how to handle it. Even if the solution is bare-bones, it gives the entire team something to build on.

I used to tell my teams, "If you don't have time to think of a solution, why do you think I have time to listen to your problem?" I meant it, but I said it with all the kindness I have in my heart. My job as a leader isn't to babysit every monkey in the business. My job is to create a culture where the people closest to the issue are trusted and expected to solve it. That's how you build real traction.

Don't leave your team sitting in the middle of the trail with a bike chain off its tracks, waiting for someone else to fix it. Teach them how to at least try to put it back on. That effort is where growth begins.

Before we go any farther, it's important to recognize the reality that team members aren't the only ones who struggle with worshiping the problem. Sometimes it's just as difficult for leadership to give up control. But if you want a problem-solving culture—and I promise you do—you have to stop grabbing the monkey.

The Reality: Stop Passing the Monkey

A lot of leaders struggle to give up control of all the monkeys and end up stealing the opportunity for growth from their teams. They lay down the rule—don't present a problem without offering a solution—but then they can't help themselves. The first time somebody brings a half-baked idea as a solution, the leader says, "Move over and let me handle this." The monkey jumps to the wrong shoulders, and the team member loses out on the chance for growth. And you know what that leads to? Cultural mediocrity.

Cultural Mediocrity

Cultural mediocrity doesn't show up overnight. It sneaks in through small compromises one monkey at a time. Every time a leader takes the monkey back instead of pushing it down the right branch, the system dulls a little. Team members stop stretching and growing because they don't have to. Standards start slipping. Before long, you've built a business that runs at 92% of its potential and calls it good.

I have found that mediocrity practically has a smell. I can walk into a meeting and sense it right away. The energy inside the office is low, the vision and goals are vague, and there's no sense of urgency. Everyone's busy, but nothing's moving. Ownership disappears from the structure, and the only movement you see is of monkeys bouncing up the chain and slowing everything down. That's not acceptable. So what do you do?

As the business leader, it's your job to hate mediocrity enough to call it out. You've got to be the pied piper against it. Walk through the business and root out mediocrity everywhere it hides. Because if you don't, it becomes the standard your structure is built on, and that standard is weak. Most companies don't fail because of big, dramatic blowups. They fail because mediocrity became acceptable. "Good enough" crept into the culture and stayed.

Compare the two images of a runner below. Look at the emphasis on starting line and finish line related to percent of goal. What is the difference? Could this simple difference in mindset, approach, and expectation catapult performance in your culture? Yes it can!

In simplest terms, we start doing our job at 100% of the goal. This one cultural shift can transform a team!

In the first picture the runner starts doing his job at 0% and finishes doing his job at 100% of the goal. That is mediocrity. Why settle for doing what everyone else does? In the second picture the runner starts doing his job at 100% of goal and will far exceed 100%. This is excellence.

Teach your people to start doing their jobs at 100% of the goal. This one cultural shift can transform a team. Expect 100% of daily, weekly, monthly, quarterly and annual goals to be exceeded. This creates a culture of winning. Winners exceed expectations, and they do it at every level. Winners recover from mistakes and errors and come back with a hard swing. Winners see their role and success as surpassing goals. So winners do not feel they have done their job until they surpass 100%.

So when I talk about structure, this is what I mean. Structure isn't just lines on an org chart—it's the backbone that either supports excellence or props up mediocrity. You can't build a high-performing team on a foundation that tolerates average.

If you want overachievement, you've got to start by expecting the team to start at 100%, not perform up to it.

And you can start by resisting the urge to take on someone else's job. Doing so is the equivalent of doing your kid's homework. They'll never learn to think for themselves if you do it for them, and you'll end up with a company full of adults who act like kids, waiting for mom or dad to fix it. That's not leadership. That's enablement.

If reading that makes you feel uncomfortable because it hits close to home, you're not alone. And it's not too late to change. Here's how:

1. **Hand the monkey back.** Let accountability for the problem remain where the problem originated by asking, "What would *you* do?"

2. **Approve ideas and implementation quickly.** Don't make people jump through hoops.

3. **Don't micromanage.** Once the problem is on someone else's shoulders, hands off unless they ask for help.

4. **Don't steal the win.** When someone solves a problem—even if it's clumsy—recognize the effort and celebrate it.

You have to be willing to let people fail. Not catastrophic failure, of course, but the kind of small stumbles that teach better than any lecture could. Every time someone fixes their own problem, they grow. And when your people grow, your company grows.

So as a leader, stop carrying monkeys that don't belong to you. You don't have time to solve every problem in the business.

And even if you did, that wouldn't be leading. That would be babysitting. And *nobody* gets paid enough to wrangle a whole zoo full of monkeys.

Requiring your team members to solve their own problems doesn't mean you should throw your people in the deep end without a life jacket. To help your team wrangle their own monkeys successfully, make sure they're equipped to succeed with the tools and structures they need. Let me introduce you to one of my favorites.

Equip Your Teams to Succeed

One of the best systems I've ever used for helping team members quickly prioritize and solve issues is the IDS tool from EOS, the Entrepreneurial Operating System, as described by Gino Wickman in his book *Traction: Get a Grip on Your Business.*[6] IDS stands for Identify, Discuss, Solve and is a simple yet powerful way to turn a business meeting into a problem-solving session. Here's how it works:

Step 1: Make a list of issues.

Step 2: Prioritize the top three.

Step 3: Brainstorm solutions for the top three by identifying the real root issues.

Step 4: Break each solution into clear to-dos and assign to specific people

Step 5: Check back in on their progress the next week.

---

[6] Wickman, *Traction*, 176.

To really transform your culture, two-thirds of every meeting should be spent on problem-solving. When you spend this much time creating solutions, things start getting done. People stop walking away drained and start walking away energized. They know they're making progress instead of just swapping monkeys. Make sure the team is clear that this is problem-solving time. You're not admiring issues or kicking them up to leadership. You're actually creating solutions for them.

The IDS tool accomplishes two things: (1) It promotes accountability, and (2) it teaches users how to work problems down into bite-sized chunks. Most problems aren't solved in one swing of the axe. You've got to keep chopping week after week until the tree falls.

So if you want a business full of problem solvers, set them up for success. Give them the tools, the skill sets, and the authority to act, then hold them accountable to use it. The IDS tool is the tip of the iceberg when it comes to giving your team the structure and tools they need to become a problem-solving team. In the next chapter, I'm going to go more in depth on the kind of structure that facilitates problem solving best. But for now, just know that with the right tools, anyone on your team can rise to the occasion and become a problem solver.

Problem Solving in Action

Just how powerful is problem solving? It's so powerful that even one problem solver on your team can make a huge difference. One of my favorite examples of problem solving in action came from an interaction I had with a janitor. This guy worked nights cleaning our retail locations. He was a really great guy and did his job well. Most of the time, he did his job under the radar, and nobody thought twice about him. Then one evening when I happened to be on location working late, he knocked on my office door.

"Excuse me, sir," he said. "Can I talk to you for a minute?"

"Yeah, sure!" I said. "What can I do for you?"

"There's some stuff going on that you should know about. The way the sales floor employees leave this place at night has got to be costing you money."

"Oh yeah? What's going on?"

He laid it out. The cash drawers weren't being reconciled at the end of the night. Workers were leaving pagers and inventory out, theft was up, and he was finding gum and cigarette burns in the carpet.

"Oh, man. Yeah, that's not good. Thank you for bringing this to my attention. Why haven't I heard about this before?"

"I told my manager over and over again, but nothing ever changes," he said.

I wasn't happy to hear that. None of this was his fault. These issues should have been brought to my attention long ago, and he was just trying to do what was right.

"Well, what would *you* do?" I asked.

The list of action items he rattled off were simple, commonsense fixes. We talked for over an hour. I learned that he had a lot of business experience from owning a barber shop for years. The cleaning company he ran now was his retirement activity.

"Those are great suggestions!" I said as I thanked him for his insight. "You have my word that things are going to change."

And change they did. The next time the head of retail sales from multiple locations came in, I was knocking on *his* door.

"You know," I said. "I was talking to the janitor at the downtown location the other night, and he did your job for you. He told me about problems happening on the retail floor—things you haven't told me about. And he gave me some good solutions."

The color drained out of his face as I talked. I wasn't done yet.

"So here's what you're going to do. You're going to go implement all of these solutions for him. And if it works, we're gonna bonus him $1,000 at Christmas."

"Out of my bonus?" he asked, looking like he was about to cry.

"No, I'm not going to take it out of yours. But we've got 20 retail locations, and if we're losing money because this is happening at all 20 of them, then a thousand bucks is nothing if it gets fixed."

To the credit of the head of retail sales, he did it. And it worked. Theft dropped, cash reconciled, and the stores looked better. And that janitor—a team member most people overlooked— ended up teaching all of us something about ownership and solutions.

That's the power of letting problems be solved where they live. Solutions don't always come from the corner office. They come from the people closest to the pain. But what happens when a problem can't be solved where it was found?

Escalation Done Right

Not every problem can be solved where it's uncovered. Some problems will require intervention from higher up the chain. Don't leave your team feeling like they're stuck dealing with something they're not allowed to deal with. Issues that involve the following need to be escalated to leadership:

- Human resources issues
- Financial risks
- Hiring or firing decisions
- Purchases that require higher clearance approval

When an issue needs escalation, encourage your team members to first brainstorm solutions. That way when the problem gets passed up to a leader, it doesn't land as dead weight. It lands with momentum. It lands with a running start.

Supervisors have a critical role here. They're the ones who facilitate the transfer of problems by first helping their people map out solutions, then adding their own input and carrying the situation to the right person. By the time a problem reaches the VP's office, it should already have two or three potential solutions attached.

After a problem has been assessed, sometimes it'll flow back down. That's fine. The goal is always to keep problems at the lowest level where they can reasonably be solved. This time, though, the problem will come back with the right permissions and resources behind it. Escalation is not about dumping responsibility; it's about getting the right people in the fight without stripping ownership away from the folks closest to the pain.

Escalation done right is one way to help a problem-solving culture stick. Now let's talk about a few more things that can help your team shift from problem worshiping to problem solving.

Making It Stick

If you really want to shift your culture from problem worshiping to problem solving, you've got to celebrate solutions, not just point out problems. That means when somebody takes ownership, tries an idea, and makes progress, you recognize it. Ring the bell. Tell the story. Call it out in front of their peers. That kind of recognition spreads faster than any memo ever will. It lights a fire in your culture. People realize their ideas matter, and they stop passing monkeys up the chain and start chasing solutions.

And don't make the mistake of stealing their win. Leaders who take credit for their team's ideas kill initiative. When your people solve problems, spotlight them. Say, "This was Janice's solution" or "Steve came up with this fix." Give the credit away. It costs you nothing, and it makes your culture worth a fortune.

When people feel valued and celebrated, they know they matter. They realize they're not just cogs in the wheel. They're thinkers, builders, and problem-solvers. Their confidence goes up. Promotions start happening because people are ready for more. The business gets faster and sharper when problems get solved where they happen instead of bottlenecking at the top.

Comfortably Miserable vs. Growth-Oriented

Like I said above, not everyone will make the shift from problem worshiper to problem solver. Some folks would rather stay comfortably miserable. They'll sit in meetings, gripe about what's broken, and even fight you when you ask them to think about solutions. Why? Because misery is familiar. It feels safer than the discomfort of change—even if that change would make things better.

The comfortably miserable people in a business remind me of a Geico commercial where a group of 20-somethings are running from a serial killer. As they search for a place to hide, one of them spies a shed full of old tools.

"Let's hide in the shed with all the chainsaws!" he shouts.

"Nooooooo!" you yell at the television screen. It's no mystery how this is going to end. That's what it's like working with comfortably miserable people—they'd rather camp out in dysfunction than face the stretch of solving problems.

The hard truth is, if they refuse to grow, they've got to go. You can't build a problem-solving culture while tolerating people who only worship the problem. In the long run, they'll drag everyone else down.

On the other hand, when you get a team that leans into solving problems, the growth is unstoppable. People gain confidence, earn promotions, and step into bigger challenges. Leaders finally get to focus on the work only they can do. And the company becomes the kind of place where energy flows forward instead of getting stuck in complaint cycles.

Making the Shift

At the end of the day, business is nothing more than solving problems for a profit. If all your team is doing is calling out problems, pushing them up the ladder, and waiting on somebody else to fix them, that's not business. That's a one-way ticket to burnout for your leadership.

The shift from a problem-worshiping culture to a problem-solving culture is one of the most powerful transformations you can help your business's culture make. It starts with a simple rule: no problem without a solution. Then it's reinforced by leaders who refuse to grab monkeys, by tools and systems that equip people to act, and by a culture that celebrates effort and ownership instead of complaint.

When your people grow in their ability to solve problems, your company grows right alongside them. Meetings get shorter, decisions get faster, and opportunities don't slip away. Most importantly, your team learns to think—and that's what you've been paying them for all along.

Shifting your culture from problem worship to problem solving is a game changer. But it won't stick without the right structure to hold it up. You can have the best intentions, the sharpest people, and the clearest rules, but if the business is leaning like a crooked barn, those monkeys will still find their way back to your shoulders.

That's why having a strong structure in your business is so important. Before you worry about who's in which role, you've got to make sure the structure itself is solid. Like you wouldn't build a house around the furniture, you can't build a company around personalities. In the next chapter, I'll show you how to design the right structure first and *then* put the right people in the right seats.

Chapter 7

Structure First, People Second

Too many companies try to build their structures around the people they already have. They look at Bob or Sally and say, "We really like them. We'll design the role around what they're good at." Sounds like a good idea, but that's backwards. Building your business around people is like building a fort around granddad's rocking chair. No matter how much you love that rocking chair, if the walls aren't fortified and the foundation is cracked, that fort won't hold.

Businesses work the same way. They need a solid structure with defined roles, clear responsibilities, and disciplined meeting rhythms *before* you start plugging people into it. Otherwise you end up with a leaning building and a whole lot of confusion. When the structure's wrong, even great people can't win.

Back in the 1990s, when I was getting my master's degree at the University of Alabama, I had a professor named Dr. Petty. He wasn't just good, he was the best professor I ever had. And he drilled this one core principle over and over: *structure first, people second.* That principle stuck with me then, and it's still one of the most important lessons I've ever learned about building businesses.

So if you want a culture where problems actually get solved, not just worshiped, you've got to start here. You've got to build the structure first. Then—and only then—do you go looking for the right people to fill the seats.

Why Structure First Matters

I've seen plenty of leaders beat their heads against the wall because their team can't get traction. They've got smart people who are hard workers and loyal employees. And yet nothing's moving the way it should. Many times, it's not the people. It's the structure.

Even the best people can't succeed inside a broken system. You can take an A player and drop them into a role that isn't clearly defined, and even they will spin their wheels until they burn out. On the flip side, if you take a decent player and give them a crystal clear role with the right structure behind it, they'll thrive.

Structure isn't optional. Structure is the foundation.

Picture a fort out West. The fort is there to protect the civilians so they can safely provide for their families. One day, as the dust blows and the sun beats down, a band of outlaws rides over the ridge. If the gates of the fort sag or the walls wobble, it doesn't matter how many rifles you've got inside. One good shove and the whole thing falls. The fort needs to have a strong foundation.

And so does your business. Structure is the difference between a business that leans, lists, and lurches along and one that stands straight, scales, and solves problems at every level.

Overcoming Intimidation

Most businesses live in the current state instead of reaching for the optimal state. They look at the org chart as it currently exists then copy and paste it forward, even if it's not working. Deadlines are missed, customer satisfaction is low, and teams aren't working well together. Everyone ends up comfortably miserable, living with mediocrity, because it feels easier than tearing it down and doing it right.

In my experience, most leaders drag their feet on building structure. They know it's important, but it feels daunting. Sitting down to map out roles, responsibilities, and accountabilities looks like a mountain of work, so they kick the can down the road.

I get it. I've done it myself. You look at that blank page and think, *I don't have time to do this right now.* But every week you delay, you're paying the price in confusion, wasted effort, and frustration. You're living with a leaning stockade because you're too intimidated to grab a hammer.

The truth is, structure doesn't have to be complicated. The hardest part is starting. Once you do, you'll realize this isn't some impossible project. It's common sense, written down and agreed upon. And the clarity it creates is worth every ounce of effort.

Ready? Stick with me as I give you a simple framework for getting structure right.

The Accountability Chart

One of the best tools I've ever found for getting structure right comes from something I learned from Entrepreneur Operating System (EOS).[7] It's called an Accountability Chart. It's similar to an org chart, but it simplifies the process so it's less intimidating. It doesn't only tell you who reports to whom. It tells you what matters most in every single role.

You can visit the book website listed in the Resources section of this book to download my fillable Accountability Chart. Or, if you like, grab a sheet of paper. Here's how you build one.

Step 1: Write the role title at the top of the page.

Step 2: Underneath, list no more than ten bullet points that outline the most vital functions of that role. Seven or fewer is even better.

Those bullet points represent the 20% of effort that drives 80% of the results for that role. The 80/20 rule is always at play. If a role has ten responsibilities, two or three of them carry the most weight. Don't fill your chart with fluff. Get laser focused on what *really* moves the needle.

Take the CEO role, for example. The big rock's vital role isn't going to be "answer emails" or "approve PTO." They're things like: manage and hold accountable the C-level team, align the vision with execution, work with the board, and lead major funding or strategic initiatives. That's it. If the CEO does the

---

[7] Wickman, *Traction.*

few things you list for them well, the business wins. Everything else is noise.

Start building out your Accountability Chart from the top down. And don't think you have to figure this out for every role in the company. Your department heads should build out the roles in their departments. They're the ones closest to the work, so they know what's essential. Your job is to make sure every department builds their chart and then "true it up" so the whole structure holds together.

That's how you create clarity. That's how you stop people from bumping into each other, duplicating work, or dropping balls because nobody knows who's on the hook. The Accountability Chart takes away the guesswork and makes sure everybody knows exactly what's expected and how their role fits into the bigger picture. But what should the big picture look like when you're talking about your company's organization? It should be as flat as possible.

Be as Flat as Possible

Once you've built your Accountability Chart, step back and take a 30,000-foot view of what it really says about your organization. One of the biggest mistakes leaders make is either layering on too much management or providing not enough. This is where you separate the frontier towns from the forts. The best practice is to be as flat as possible while still maintaining a healthy span of control.

Think of your business like a frontier outpost. You don't want so many captains that the soldiers don't know who to salute;

you also don't want one poor lieutenant trying to command every sentry on the wall. Too many layers and you slow down decision-making until it feels like sending a telegram across three territories. Too few layers and you stretch your leaders so thin they can't protect the fort. You want to be lean but not starving.

A good rule of thumb is that no one should have more than eight to ten people directly reporting to them. Any more than that, and you start breaking the laws of organizational physics. When one person is managing 20 or 30 people, these things happen every time:

1. Consistency issues: You lose your ability to stay "on brand." Standards drift, and different teams start doing things their own way.

2. Time issues: There's simply no time to meet with everyone, communicate well, or develop your people.

3. Performance issues: When communication breaks down, the bar quietly lowers. Mediocrity creeps in.

4. Burnout: Even your strongest leaders eventually collapse under that kind of load. If you've got a manager carrying 20 direct reports, don't praise them—protect them. Build a layer underneath to split the weight before you lose them.

On the other side of the spectrum, a manager with only three direct reports probably isn't needed. You're paying for management that isn't managing enough people to justify the cost.

The goal is to keep a good balance. Two managers overseeing 15 people total or 2:15 is a healthy ratio. One manager over 15 people (a 1:15 ratio) is too flat. The 2:15 sweet spot allows for accountability without excess overhead.

You'll also want to look at the geography of your company. Do your managers actually live where their teams are? If you've got someone in Chicago managing people in Alabama, ask yourself how that's working out. Geography matters more than most people realize. Leaders should be close enough to their teams to coach, visit, and problem-solve without burning time or travel budgets to be present.

When you evaluate structure, don't overcomplicate it. Just ask:

- How many people does each manager manage?
- Is that number working?
- Are managers positioned where they can lead effectively?

That's the *flat but strong* principle, and it ensures companies will be lean, logical, and built for performance. Many companies end up with bloated management, illogical territories, or spans of control that make no sense. But with the right leadership roles in the right locations, managing the right number of people, your company can scale without sagging.

People Second

Once you've nailed down the structure with your Accountability Chart, only *then* do you look at the people. This is where most businesses get it backwards. They start with faces and names, then bend the structure to fit whoever's on the payroll. Think about it though. Remember, you don't design the fort around the lookouts on the wall. You design the fort first, then place the lookouts.

It's simple but not easy. The hard part is that when you build structure first, you're going to realize not everybody fits. Some people will line up perfectly with the role they're in and others won't. You're going to have decisions to make.

You've got a few options:

- If a role truly isn't needed anymore, eliminate it. Keep the best players in the seats that matter.
- If someone's strengths fit another seat, repurpose them— only if it makes real sense for the business, not just because you like them.
- If the team member doesn't fit the culture or the role, you may need to part ways.

What you can't do is invent roles to hang on to people you're attached to. Keeping someone on payroll who isn't delivering because it feels easier than making the hard call is how you end up comfortably miserable. And I promise you, that pain compounds over time.

The Pain and Payoff

Let's not sugarcoat it. Building structure first is hard. It's hard if you're a startup sketching roles on a blank sheet of paper, and it's hard if you're an established business with people already in seats. Either way, there's pain involved.

You might have to eliminate a role. You might have to move someone you like into a different seat or out of the business altogether. It won't feel good in the moment. People will whisper, "Can you believe they let Bob go?" You'll second-guess yourself. But the truth is, you're going to pay the piper one way or another. You'll either pay by facing the discomfort of fixing it now, or you'll pay by dragging mediocrity around for years and letting it quietly bleed your business dry.

But if you do the work—if you build the structure, then fill the seats—you'll experience the payoff that comes after the pain. Once the structure is strong and the right people are in the right seats, the whole business breathes easier. People will operate well within their outlined roles. Accountability is clear, and frustration levels drop.

When you do the work, you prove to your team that structure first, people second actually works. That's how you build trust. Every time you fix a structural issue and it makes life better, your people will be more willing to follow you down the narrow, less-traveled trail of best practice.

Once you have your positions outlined and seats filled (more on getting the right people in the right seats in chapter 11), it's time to turn your attention to the day-to-day business operations. And for that, you're going to want to make sure you have a disciplined meeting rhythm.

Meeting Rhythms as Part of Structure

One of the biggest structural game changers you can put in place in your business is a disciplined meeting rhythm. I recommend having a weekly meeting pulse. What do I mean by that?

Every department in your business should have a weekly meeting. And when I say weekly meeting, I'm not talking about a sit around the campfire and shoot the breeze type of meeting. I'm talking about an intentional, problem-solving meeting. The kind that should tie back to your quarterly goals, which roll into your annual plan. That way every conversation is connected to where your wagon train is headed.

As I mentioned in chapter 6, two-thirds of your meeting time should be dedicated to solving problems. Pick the top issues, tackle them one at a time, assign clear to-dos, and move forward.

If your meeting isn't solving problems, it's a waste of time. In fact, I've told teams, "If you're in a meeting that's not solving problems, you have my permission to walk out." That'll wake folks up in a hurry.

Structure your meetings so they drive accountability, create momentum, and keep problems from piling up at the top. I'll give you more tips on effective meetings in chapter 8. For now, just know that when meetings become engines of problem solving, your culture shifts from *talking* about issues to *fixing* them. That's structure in action, which is important to note because structure is never done.

Continuous Process

Businesses aren't static. They grow, shrink, pivot, and hit bumps in the road. If your business is alive, your structure has to evolve with it.

At a minimum, you should review your structure once a year. Call it a sanity check. Pull out your Accountability Chart and ask yourself if it still makes sense. Are the right roles defined the right way? Are the right people in the right seats? If not, fix it.

But you don't have to wait 12 months if a structural issue shows up sooner. I strongly encourage you to adjust things structurally as issues present themselves. A lot of times, you'll uncover the root cause of a problem in a weekly or quarterly meeting, and it won't be the person—it'll be the structure. When that happens, adjust on the fly. Don't let it sit and fester because the calendar says you're not due for a review.

Leadership takes discipline. It takes choosing to stop settling for being comfortably miserable, face reality, and make corrections. Over time those small course adjustments add up to a company that runs straighter, faster, and stronger.

Structure isn't a onetime project; it's a constant process. But once you commit to the structure, the payoff is a business that doesn't only survive change, it thrives on it.

Going Deeper

Structure first, people second isn't just a catchy phrase. Structure is the backbone of a business that actually works. When you build the structure first, you create clarity. Everyone knows their role, their responsibilities, and how success gets measured. When you put the right people in those clearly defined seats, you create traction. Vision and subvision gets passed on all the way to the bottom. Problems get solved where they happen, meetings drive action, and accountability becomes part of the culture.

Is it easy? No. You'll face tough calls, you'll feel the pain of change, and you'll probably tick some people off along the way. But every time you fix a structural issue and see the business run smoother, you prove that best practice beats mediocrity. Over time those wins build trust, momentum, and a culture that refuses to settle for comfortably miserable.

Businesses that ignore structure end up leaning, listing, and lurching their way forward. Businesses that get structure right stand tall, move fast, and scale without breaking. So if you want a company that solves problems instead of worshiping them, start here. Build the fort first, then fill it with the right people.

Getting the structure right doesn't only steady the wagon. It also changes the way your whole outfit communicates. Once roles are clear and the fort is built strong, you'll notice a new problem creeping up in how people use that structure day-to-day. A lot of leaders get tripped up here. Even with the right chart on the wall, accountability still gets lost in the shuffle when folks rely on bad habits to pass information around.

One of the worst offenders is drive-by meeting culture, where people abuse the popular open door policy many leaders have and stop by unannounced throughout the day to offload their problems. There's not much that's more disruptive than having to field a half dozen drop-ins throughout the day. One minute you're making your way steadily down the trail and the next, you're sidelined by somebody poking their head in your office with "Got a second?" By the time they leave, you're carrying another monkey on your back.

Meetings are necessary. But drive-by meetings are chaos disguised as communication. Next up, I'm going to show you how to ditch the drive-by meeting culture and how to structure meetings for productivity and problem-solving.

Chapter 8

Drive-By Meeting Culture

On a dusty main street in a frontier town, all is quiet. The sheriff's cleaning his gun, and his deputies are out on patrol. The townsfolk are milling around, chatting outside the general store and running errands. Suddenly, out of nowhere, a cowboy barrels down the center of the street on horseback, firing shots in the air and hollering for the sheriff.

He reins in his horse next to the jail and vaults himself out of the saddle.

"Sheriff! Sheriff! I was out riding the range, and I got to thinkin' that there might be some rustlers up in them there hills. What are we gonna do? What if they come for the cattle? What if they come for the townsfolk? You gotta do something!"

Before anybody can make sense of what he's saying or what he wants, he launches himself back in the saddle and rides off, leaving a cloud of dust in his wake. The peace of the town is broken, leaving everyone rattled and unsure what's going on, the sheriff especially. He's supposed to just drop everything and solve a problem that might or might not exist?

You've just experienced a wild west version of a drive-by meeting. There was a whole lot of action and a whole lot of urgency…but all it left behind was chaos and confusion. Who's holding the monkey now?

The irony is this drive-by meeting practice comes from well-intentioned clichés you can read in many business development books. Leaders are told to keep their office doors open and be accessible to their people. And of course, there is value in those practices. As a leader, you should be present. You should have an eye on what's happening in the trenches.

But none of that trumps good organization.

If you let openness turn into "anyone can interrupt anyone at any time," you're not leading. You're doing the equivalent of running a wild west town with no law. You're letting monkeys jump from shoulder to shoulder without reason. Sooner or later, somebody's gonna get waylaid, and it might be *you*.

This chapter is about putting an end to drive-by meeting culture. We're going to define what drive-by meetings are, why they destroy accountability and focus, and—most important—what to replace them with if you want speed and trust in your business. If you don't replace drive-by meetings with structure, chaos will keep running the show, and your show will keep running off the rails.

Drive-By Meeting Culture Defined

One of the most ominous phrases a business leader can hear in the middle of their working day is, "Hey, you got a minute?" Drive-by meetings are unexpected occurrences that are impossible to plan for. They happen when someone ambushes you in the hallway, pokes their head through your office door, or corners you by the coffee pot.

The problem with these "Got a minute?" chats is that they're hardly ever quick. And they're hardly ever without complication. More often than not, a drive-by meeting ends with you holding a new monkey while the other guy rides off into the sunset before you can even get a good look at what you've been saddled with.

While an open-door policy may sound noble, in practice, it turns your business into Dodge City on a Saturday night. Deputies abandon their posts to deal with last-minute complaints. Accountability gets fuzzy. Before long, nobody knows who is handling which problem, or if anybody's handling them at all.

Drive-by meetings only create the *illusion* of progress. The visiting party feels better since they metaphorically plucked the monkey off their shoulders and placed it onto yours. But nothing got solved. There's no opportunity for planning, context, or clarity. And that's a problem. Allowing drive-by meeting culture to take root in your company isn't leadership—it's chaos with a badge.

Why Drive-Bys Break the Business

Drive-by meetings look harmless. If somebody needs a "quick word," what is wrong with that? The problem may be hard to see on the surface, yet beneath it lies one of the most destructive habits a company can tolerate. Here are the reasons why.

Drive-By Meetings Interrupt Thought

Thinking is a company leader's highest priority. Strategy, planning, and creative problem-solving are literally your job, but none of that can happen when your focus gets ambushed multiple times a day. Drive-by meetings break your concentration, and once your train of thought derails, it can take hours to recover.

Drive-By Meetings Destroy Accountability

Drive-bys meeting culture creates a "monkey jumping" issue. An employee enters, tosses their monkey (problem) to the leader, then leaves. They think to themselves, *I told my boss, so he'll take care of it.* But will he? Will anyone? In reality, during drive-by meetings there's no time to assign tasks or create a plan, so everybody walks away confused.

Drive-By Meetings Give the Illusion of Effectiveness

Like shuffling monkeys from shoulder to shoulder, allowing your people to shift responsibilities onto leaderships' shoulders feels good at the moment—at least it does to the employee. Their shoulders feel lighter, but it's a false handoff. Without context or a plan, no progress gets made. The only thing that really happens is a mess gets handed up the line.

Drive-By Meetings Create Bad Etiquette and Misuse of Power

So far we've only addressed the employee-to-leader dynamic of drive-by meetings. But it works the other way too—leader to employee—and it's just as damaging. When a boss drops casual orders in passing, employees tend to scramble to obey, even if it wrecks priorities set by their manager. That's not leadership; that's chaos disguised as authority.

Drive-By Meetings Breed Mistrust

Pretend you're an employee sitting in a cubicle across the hall from your manager. All day long, other team members stream in and out of his office to pick his brain. In the process, they air out all kinds of issues that probably don't need to be discussed at that time. How do you know? Because the door is open. You can hear it all.

If you were that employee, the last thing you'd feel safe doing is bringing something to your leader. An open door without boundaries quickly becomes an "open season" where nothing feels safe or private.

Left unchecked, drive-by meetings chip away at the very things a business needs most: focus, trust, and accountability. They leave good people looking unresponsive, leaders frustrated by dropped balls, and whole teams wasting time chasing problems that were never theirs to begin with.

"Hey, Call Me"

I've seen drive-by meeting culture play out more times than I can count. One of the clearest examples I ever experienced was when I was working with EBSCO, a $4 billion holding company. I was brought in to help turn around several business units within the company that weren't hitting results—and these weren't small problems. Whole teams were floundering, good people were burning out, and ownership was getting frustrated.

And surprise, surprise, the core of the dysfunction was drive-by meetings. People were sending emails that said nothing more than "Hey, call me." Managers were ambushing each other in hallways with random requests. Bosses were dropping casual orders that yanked employees off their priorities. It was chaos in boots.

So I did something simple but radical: I outlawed drive-bys. I rolled up my sleeves and sat in on meetings myself, sitting shoulder to shoulder with the department heads to lay out the new standards.

First, I explained the concept of passing the monkey based on the *Harvard Business Review* article mentioned in chapter 6 and told them there would be no more passing monkeys around.[8] If you've got an issue, bring it to the weekly meeting. Then, I taught them how to request time when they needed help. I showed them the three-sentence structure (explained in the section below) so the other person would know exactly what they needed, how urgent it was, and when they expected to follow up.

And you know what happened when I finished laying it out? They were relieved! You could feel the tension in the room break. They even laughed when I read their old voicemails aloud and they heard the "Hey man, call me" line. Within a week, the culture had shifted. Suddenly problems were being documented, prioritized, and solved. People learned they could trust the system and that their issue would get airtime within seven days.

------

[8] Oncken Jr. and Wass, "Management Time," *Harvard Business Review.*

I've walked into companies that felt like lawless frontier towns, where every day was a shootout of random requests. And I've watched those same places settle into order once we put structure in place. Drive-by meeting culture is one of the biggest dysfunctions in business, yet the easiest one to fix if you've got the backbone to do it. So how *do* you fix it?

Replacing Chaos with Structure

So how do you fix this? Well, you can't just outlaw drive-bys and expect the problem to disappear. If you take away a bad habit, you have to replace it with a better one. Otherwise, people will fall back into the same patterns. Here's how I help business leaders leave drive-by-meeting culture behind.

First, define what counts as a true drive-by meeting.

Not all drive-by meetings are created equal. There are a two no-appointment-needed reasons to interrupt someone's day:

Emergencies: Anytime there's a health crisis, safety concern, or urgent personal issue.

Celebrations: When you land a big client or hit a milestone worth sharing.

That's it. If something doesn't fall into one of those buckets, it's not a permissible drive-by meeting. It belongs on the calendar. And if you do happen to be in the middle of an emergency or a win, the emergency or win is the sole focus. No monkey passing allowed.

Second, train your people in the three-sentence structure.

When employees need some of your time, they can ask for it quickly and succinctly in three sentences—what I call the three-sentence structure. This provides clarity and a timeline, two things that keep things on the rails and help you prioritize the issue appropriately.

Briefly state the issue: "I'm having a conflict with one of my clients and need your advice."

Give a clear indicator of urgency: "We need to close on their deal soon."

Provide a timeframe for follow-up: "If I could have 15 minutes of your time before Friday, that would be great."

The three-sentence structure is respectful and gives context, urgency, and a window to respond. Imagine getting a request in the three-sentence structure compared to the usual "Hey, we need to talk." One builds trust. The other builds panic. I know which request I prefer. How about you?

Third, build a dependable weekly meeting pulse.

If you want to kill drive-bys, you've got to create law and order in the way your team solves problems. Give them an outlet so they feel heard, but don't let every interaction around the watering hole get hijacked.

In chapter 7, we discussed what a good weekly meeting pulse looks like. Here's a quick review within the context of how this helps prevent drive-by meeting culture from taking over.

Weekly Meeting Best Practices

- Hold a 90-minute meeting at the same time and same place every week.
- Require everyone to be present with phones off and laptops closed.
- Devote the first 30 minutes to reviewing scorecards, dashboards, and vital signs of the company. Review the to-dos from last week's meeting
- In the remaining 60 minutes, handle the issues. Put them in priority order, then work through them using the IDS (identify, discuss, solve) framework discussed in chapter 7.
- Create a concrete to-do list for each issue.
- Assign the to-dos to someone in the room who will take responsibility for acting on them within the next 7 days.
- That person will take action, then report on their progress in the first 30 minutes of the next weekly meeting.

See how this rhythm removes the need for drive-by meetings? When your employees know they have a set time to address their issues, they'll stop ambushing you and each other in the hallway. They know their issue will get airtime at the next meeting.

Roll out weekly meetings through the chain of command.
In a large company, each department needs its own weekly meeting, starting at the C-suite level. For example you will meet weekly with the people directly below you. Then those people—your manager or directors—will meet with the

people directly below them, and so on all the way down to the janitorial staff.

You, as the leader, need to model this meeting structure first. If the C-suite doesn't follow it, no one else will. Stay accountable to fulfilling the weekly meeting best practices and the three-sentence structure. Being the boss doesn't give you permission to derail other people's priorities with low-importance "while you're at it" requests.

Replacing drive-by meetings with structured weekly meetings gives a lawless town a schedule and a code to follow. Instead of chaos, everyone knows where to bring their problems, how they'll be handled, and who's accountable for fixing them.

And when that happens, the business will finally start to move at the speed it's supposed to.

Build Trust Through Communication

Drive-by meeting culture thrives in the dark. When people don't know what's happening with their issue, they fill in the blanks with their own assumptions. And we all know what happens when you assume. You rarely ever get a positive outcome.

So there's one more vital component to ditching drive-by meeting culture for good. It's not enough to outlaw drive-bys and put a meeting pulse in place. You've also got to circle back. Sometimes the answer to someone's concern will be, "We're not going to act on this right now." That's fine. Doing nothing is a legitimate decision. But that has to be communicated to the person who brought the issue to the table. Otherwise people feel ignored, and ignored people go right back to ambushing each other in the hallway.

Leaders build trust not by solving every single problem, but by being clear about what will be done and what won't. If you choose not to act, say so. If something gets tabled, explain why. That communication alone lowers anxiety and keeps people from jumping the fence and tossing their monkeys up the chain of command.

When you replace the chaos of drive-bys with structure, discipline, and respect, you'll see the shift almost immediately. Your team will stop living in reaction mode, and accountability will stick. Your business will finally start running like a town with law and order where people know where to go, how things get handled, and who's responsible for what.

That's how you end drive-by meeting culture. Not with another slogan about being open or accessible, but with structure that creates speed and results. Ending drive-by meeting culture isn't only about stopping bad behavior. It's also about building a foundation of trust and order. When people know how issues get handled, when they'll be addressed, and who's accountable, the chaos settles. Structure takes hold.

But structure alone won't carry you all the way. Business doesn't happen in slow motion. The clock is always ticking, and windows of opportunity open and close fast. As the leader, you don't get to hit pause. That's where the next piece comes in.

Once you've built law and order in your organization, you've got to step into the role of gunslinger—the one who can see the window, draw fast, and act decisively. In the next chapter, I'll show you what being a gunslinger is all about.

Be a Gunslinger

Things move fast in the wild west of business. Windows of opportunity are always swinging open and slamming shut—sometimes even before you've finished your coffee. When it comes to a deal, a partnership, a decision, or a new hire, each one has a moment when the conditions are right. If you miss that moment and the conditions change, sometimes you lose the opportunity.

That's what I call the *speed of business.*

If you're leading a business, you can't afford to sit still and overanalyze while a dust storm blows through town or a band of outlaws coming riding through the streets. Sitting dead still is one of the most powerful mistakes you can make. A "maybe later" at the wrong time is often worse than a "no."

But don't confuse speed with recklessness. A gunslinger in business isn't the same as a cowboy shooting wildly into the street. That person puts everyone at risk. A true gunslinger knows the terrain, understands the stakes, and can draw fast *without* being careless. They get everyone through the window of opportunity and to safety with no souls left behind.

This chapter is about becoming that kind of gunslinger. Someone decisive, fast on the draw, and clear-eyed about when to say yes, when to say no, and when to hold steady. When you're that gunslinger, you'll be prepared to run a company that can move at the speed of business with a people, culture, and structure that are prepared to move right alongside you.

The Gunslinger Mindset

In your mind's eye, put yourself back in our fictional frontier town from my illustration in chapter 8. It's another peaceful morning. Birds are chirping. Children are playing in the school yard. The sheriff steps out of the jail, straightens his badge, and squints down the street. He can hear fast hoofbeats approaching. Something's coming.

Suddenly a man on a horse rounds the corner down by the livery and charges straight up Main Street towards him. As the rider gets closer, the sheriff can see that his gun is drawn and his face is hidden behind a bandana. It's an outlaw!

Now imagine that the sheriff squats in the dirt with a stick and starts calculating the angle of the sun, the wind shear, and the speed of the horse. By the time he's done with the math, it's too late. The outlaw has already robbed the bank and ridden off with a sack full of cash.

That might seem like a silly illustration. You're probably wondering why he wouldn't *do* something and thinking that you'd never make that mistake. Yet leaders do this all the time. They hesitate and overanalyze, waiting for the perfect information before acting. In a frontier town, hesitation was often fatal. And hesitation can be very detrimental in the wild west of business too.

So what does a true gunslinger act like? Well he or she isn't reckless. Gunslingers don't fire blindly into the crowd and hope for the best. They're decisive, and they know how to read the moment, make the call, and act fast enough to get their people through the window of opportunity, all without losing a soul under his or her care.

You should approach the role of gunslinger like a ship's captain. He knows how many souls are on board, and his job is to bring every one of them to shore safely. The captain accepts his responsibility to the people on his vessel. It's the same in business. Being a gunslinger isn't about showing off your sharpshooting skills. It's about protecting your team, your culture, and your company.

A gunslinger also understands the power of yes and no. Both are strong words. A decisive yes sets things in motion. A clear no keeps the business from wandering into ambush. What you can't afford is the muddled middle or the "let's wait and see" that leaves your people standing in the street while bullets fly.

Being a gunslinger is about mastering the windows—knowing when to shout "Giddy up!" and charge forward, and when to shout "Whoa!" and pull back the reins. And that takes leaning into certain qualities.

Qualities of a Gunslinger Leader

A gunslinger isn't born; he or she is forged in the dust and chaos of leading. To run at the speed of business, there are certain qualities you have to nurture in yourself and then build into your team. I've put a short list of these qualities below. For a deeper review of these qualities, refer back to chapter 4.

Quality 1: Decisiveness

Hesitation is the slow death of a business. People need to know that their leader will make the tough calls. They also need to know that they'll be trusted to make calls when the need arises. Decisiveness doesn't mean you're always right. It means you're willing to act, knowing you can course correct if needed. The confidence to decide gives everyone else the confidence to follow.

Quality 2: Fearlessness

Fearlessness doesn't equal recklessness. Fearlessness simply means you refuse to let fear keep you from pulling the trigger. You won't always have perfect data. You won't always know how it'll play out at the time the decision must be made. A gunslinger makes the best decision with the information at hand, moves forward, and adjusts when new information comes in.

Quality 3: Toughness

Leadership is a heavy, and oftentimes unbalanced, load to carry. While someone in marketing is celebrating their best week ever, one of the sales reps is dealing with the loss of your biggest customer. And you're riding herd on both. The leader carries the weight of every department's failures as well as celebrates the wins. Toughness is what keeps you upright when the load is uneven.

Quality 4: Diagnostic Skill

Being quick on the draw doesn't matter if you're aiming at the wrong problem. A gunslinger knows how to diagnose issues fast, cut through noise, and identify the real target. That means having the right reporting systems in place, the right leaders in the right seats, and the discipline to call out dysfunction before it festers.

When you portray these qualities, your people will respond with unity since they trust that you know the way through.

And you can portray these qualities to them every day by practicing connect-the-dots decision-making.

Connect-the-Dots Decision-Making

The trouble with many business leaders is they only ever think in terms of the big picture. They present the annual goal, then send their people off with a wave and "See you in 12 months!" That's like setting off for California with a wagon train and never checking the compass until you hit the ocean. Chances are, you'll end up in Mexico—or dead in the desert—instead of where you wanted to be.

That's not how a gunslinger leads. As the gunslinger, yes, you set the long-term vision. But then you break it down into quarterly, monthly, and weekly benchmarks that keep everyone pointed toward true north. As you guide your people from benchmark to benchmark, you're able to continually steer the journey in the right direction.

In that way, every decision you make is simply connecting one dot to another. That's connect-the-dots decision-making. Think of it like a trail map:

- The yearly goal is your true north—the destination at the end of the trail.
- The journey from where you are at the beginning of the year to the destination will be broken up into quarterly goals. Those are your major benchmarks along the trail.
- And in between the major benchmarks are monthly and weekly dots that connect to each other, step by step, forming a clear path ahead.

At the end of every week, you'll take a look at the map. Is everyone still on the trail heading north, or did you drift west? If you drifted even a little, you can course correct right away and keep pushing forward. In that way, the gunslinger's creed becomes *fast fail, fast fix*.

Perfection is a myth. It's impossible. Missteps and mistakes will be made. Sometimes you'll set out a strategy, and it won't work. That's fine. Really, it's okay. The *real* mistake is not practicing connect-the-dots decision-making. Instead of failing fast, realizing it, and having the opportunity to fix it fast, you'll be much farther down the trail before the problem is identified. And that becomes much more difficult and time-consuming to course correct.

But in a fast fail, fast fix culture, mistakes aren't hidden. They surface quickly so everyone can redirect and continue on with barely a missed step. Problems aren't seen as punishments. They're positioned as opportunities to adjust along the way. And wins don't require perfection. As long as everyone is moving the right way, dot-to-dot, you're winning.

It's kind of like riding a horse. You don't use your spurs until its head is pointed the right direction. And even then, as the trail zigs and zags, you carefully guide it with the reins to keep it on course. Leadership is the same—you don't wait a month to check in. By that time, you're liable to be lost in the wilderness. You check in often.

That's why simple, step-by-step strategy is critical. If the compass you hand your team has seventy-five dials, no one will be able to read it. Keep things clear by helping your people regularly analyze where they are now compared to where you said you'd be. When you run your business this way, your people stop fearing failure. They know you'll course correct quickly. They know no one gets left behind. And they learn to act at the speed of business because they see *you* doing it first.

No-Surprises Culture

One of the fastest ways to wreck trust and destroy progress in a business is surprise. And I don't mean "Surprise! It's your birthday!" I mean holding back information—good or bad—until it's too late for anyone to do something about it.

In business, surprise equals failure.

I learned that lesson the hard way. Early in my career, I landed a huge hospital account for the telecom company I worked for. It was the biggest win of my young life. I was so excited to deliver the news that I held onto it, waiting for the perfect moment to surprise my boss. I'd thought I'd blow him away with what a good job I had done. Instead I nearly got my head chewed off.

Why? Because *winning* the account was only half the story. Somebody still had to *deliver* on it, and it was no small order. The hospital needed a thousand pagers, programmed and ready, in almost no time at all. By holding back on announcing the news, I had essentially stolen time from my boss—time he could have used to prepare. What was good news to me became his logistical nightmare.

He looked me dead in the eye and said, "Mel, I have not had to teach you much, but I'm going to have to teach you this. You *never* surprise your boss in business. Ever. I don't care if it's bad news or good news. The minute you know, I need to know."

That advice stuck. To this day, I run my companies with a *no surprises* rule. That means bad news doesn't get hidden, and good news doesn't get hoarded. The moment you see smoke, you tell someone—before it's a five-alarm fire. And as you see progress develop, share it so the team can prepare for whatever comes next. No surprises means leaders don't get blindsided.

Your goal is to arrive at the end of the trail at your annual goal with everyone beside you. To keep from losing people along the way, you'll need to deal with reality at the speed of business right when it happens. Surprises—no matter which direction they come from—kill momentum, trust, and confidence. They have no place in a business.

A culture of no surprises keeps everyone aligned, builds trust, and ensures that when you call "Giddy up," the whole team can move out together without tripping over hidden problems.

When Someone *Grabs the Baby*

Every once in a while in business, you'll find yourself in what I call a *grab-the-baby* moment. It's like that scene in every Western where the outlaw storms into the saloon with his gun drawn and starts making demands. They're emotional, loud, and usually convinced they're the victim. Sometimes it's a key employee melting down. Other times it's a manager threatening to quit or a partner suddenly changing the deal. Or, like the story I told in chapter 4, sometimes it's an executive who holds the business's code over everyone's heads in order to get what he wants.

When someone grabs the baby, what should you do as the gunslinger?

First of all, don't match their emotions. Stay calm and professional, because gunslingers don't flinch. Let them talk. When they're done delivering their list of grievances or ransom demands, calmly say, "Let me make sure I have this right…" Then, restate what they said back to them as accurately and neutrally as possible. Get their 100% agreement that you heard them correctly by saying, "To confirm, this is what you're saying, right?"

Get their verbal yes or no. Once they agree, you've done two powerful things:

1. You've acknowledged them without rewarding the behavior.
2. You've documented exactly what was said at the moment.

That's double documentation—your verbal record and their confirmation. You've captured the facts while keeping your composure.

From there, discussion may or may not happen. But whether it's a hostage situation or a hard conversation, once the baby gets grabbed, gunslinger action is required. You can't freeze, but you can't get emotional either. Respond with clarity, calm, and swift, decisive leadership.

Negotiating Like a Gunslinger

Every leader becomes a negotiator at some point. It might be in a boardroom with a client or sitting across from an employee asking for a raise. And like a gunslinger in the street, the calmest hand usually wins. But after decades of deals, partnerships, and high-stakes conversations, I've learned that there's one person you should *never* negotiate with: yourself.

It's human nature to fill the silence. We automatically want to start talking if the other person doesn't respond. But in negotiation, that silence is where your strength lives. The first person to talk usually loses.

Imagine that you're buying a horse (because every good gunslinger needs a horse, right?) As you and the horse owner stand outside the corral looking at the horses he has for sale, you spot the one you want.

"I'll give you $500 for that horse," you say, pointing to a tall quarter horse with a white blaze face.

The seller follows your finger and nods but says nothing. Seconds tick away, feeling like hours. It's at this point that most people would panic and start sweetening their own deal—negotiating against themselves—before the other side even says a word.

"I can pay cash," you rush to say. "I could go a little higher."

When you negotiate with yourself, you weaken your position. Now the horse owner knows how much you want that particular animal. He's got you where he wants you, and he holds all the power.

The gunslinger approach is different. Instead of rushing to fill the silence, as a gunslinger, you wait. Let the other side feel the weight of responding; the moment you fill the silence, you're negotiating against yourself instead of for yourself.

Three Best Practices to Negotiate Like a Pro

After years of leading teams (and learning the hard way), I've boiled negotiation down to three game-changing rules:

1. Never negotiate with yourself.

Once you make an offer, stop talking. Let the other side feel the pressure. Silence is your secret weapon. Take the horse deal, for example. If I'd waited, letting dead silence fall on him after saying I'd pay $500 for that horse, the seller might've countered, saving me from bidding against myself.

2. The first to talk loses.
When you've laid out your terms, zip it. If the seller says, "That's lower than I hoped," don't bite. Stay silent or nudge them with, "What number works for you?" Force them to move the deal forward.

3. Be willing to walk away.
Power comes from knowing you can leave. If the deal feels off, the product's flawed, or the other side's unfair, walk. This mindset keeps you in control, whether you're buying a car or closing a business deal.

This principle works everywhere—in leadership, in sales, and in life. When a client says "Okay, I'll take it," you stop selling and hand them a pen. When an employee makes a demand, listen carefully, clarify what you heard, and then pause. Don't rush to fill the space or fix it too fast.

Negotiation, like gunslinging, is about timing, restraint, and nerve. You've got to be willing to wait. You've got to be willing to walk away. And you've got to know when the next move belongs to the other person.

Teach your people this discipline. Engrain "never negotiate with yourself" into your culture. Whether it's a multimillion-dollar contract or a customer complaint, your calmness in that pocket of silence communicates confidence and strength.

So what does being a gunslinger look like in the wild west of business? Well let me tell you a story…

Gunslingers in the Wild: The Actel Turnaround Attempt

The gunslinger mindset gets tested when you walk into a fight you didn't start and can't win on paper. That was me when I took a job at Actel Integrated Communications.

On the surface, Actel looked like the next AT&T. They'd burned through $65 million in venture capital, built a world-class telecom network, and plastered their brand across billboards. You couldn't drive through Alabama or Louisiana without thinking Actel was *the* telecom company.

But when I got inside, it was a ghost town. They had sales reps but no managers. There were entire markets with no one in charge. They had no structure and no gunslingers. It was chaos dressed up in good marketing.

That's when the diagnostic skill of a gunslinger came into play. I didn't have time to learn the ins and outs of telecom, and I didn't have to in order to get started. The problem was obvious to me. Without managers, the company stood no chance of long-term success. I had to hire strong managers for every market, and I had to be quick about it. I engaged a search firm, moved quickly, and filled the management roles in a matter of weeks.

In the long run, I couldn't save the business, but I came close. Before I had the chance to get them on solid ground, the economy turned, the banks panicked, and the business folded. But for a season, we pulled off the impossible. We took a company in free fall and actually hit the goals the board handed down.

How did I do it? By using the What–How–When Framework.

The What–How–When™ Framework

Out of the chaos at Actel came one of the most powerful tools I've ever developed as a leader. I didn't sit down and invent it with a whiteboard. I invented it in the middle of the fire during total survival mode. When everything's on fire, you either find a way to simplify decisions, or you get burned.

I developed a simple decision-making framework, What–How–When™, that helps achieve clarity before execution.

Here's how it works:

What

First, decide What needs to be done. Don't worry about How you'll do it or When—that comes later. If you let How creep into the conversation too early, the What gets watered down into mediocrity. At Actel, the What was clear. We had to put managers in place in every market or nothing else mattered.

How

Once the What is locked in, figure out How to make it happen. This is where creativity, resourcefulness, and grit come in. With Actel, the How was to hire fast through a retained search firm. We didn't know exactly how we'd turn sales around yet, but we knew without managers in place, there was no chance at all.

When

Only after the What and How are solid should you decide on When. Timing can kill bold ideas if you bring it up too soon. Sometimes execution has to be immediate. Other times it makes sense to wait for the right moment.

At Actel, the When was yesterday. We had no time to lose.

Focus first on a bold What, then on a relevant How. If you delay the When until those two are clear, it makes the timing of action far more accurate. Once you have several strong What-and-How combinations on the table, the When decision helps you stack them against each other. When becomes the sanity check that helps determine priority and practicality.

This is where prioritization and return on opportunity (ROO) come into play. Getting to When means you've compared every open initiative and decided what gets done first, second, third, or not at all. You've weighed impact, cost, timing, and ROO.

Opportunity cost is something every leader must teach their culture to recognize. My definition of opportunity cost is "the cost of choosing one opportunity over another." If we pick A instead of B, did we make the better call? Did we get the biggest bang for the buck? The expense isn't always in dollars—it's often in brainpower, executive focus, and energy. Every yes has a hidden no attached to it, and understanding that tradeoff is critical.

So by doing What first, then How and only then tackling When, you're setting priorities. You're making comparative, strategic choices. You're looking across the landscape of opportunities and deciding which ones deserve your horsepower now, and which ones can wait.

Of course sometimes life drops something in your lap that can't wait—like what happened with Actel. And it becomes a true speed-of-business moment. Sometimes a window opens, and you have seconds to act. In those cases, you make the call. But most of the time, this framework allows you to prioritize intelligently, sequence initiatives effectively, and avoid sinking back into mediocrity by spreading yourself too thin.

The beauty of What–How–When is that it forces clarity. This framework keeps you from backing into safe, watered-down answers because you don't yet see a clear path. It makes you name the bold move first, then marshal the resources to pull it off, and finally to slot it into the right time frame.

It's simple; but don't confuse simple with easy. The first few times you use this framework with a team, it will feel awkward. People are used to diluting the What because they're scared of not knowing the How or the When. They want to compromise early. You have to hold the line.

But once people get it, something clicks. The What gets bigger and bolder. The How gets sharper and more innovative. And the When gets more realistic since it's grounded in a solid plan.

I've used What–How–When in companies, in family decisions, and to coach my kids through tough calls. It works everywhere, whether you're running a $65 million telecom company or trying to decide your next move in life.

What is first, then How, and then When.

That's the gunslinger's way of solving problems at the speed of business.

Putting What–How–When to Work

Here's the final point: What–How–When becomes downright lethal when paired with weekly meetings that use the identify, discuss, solve (IDS) model. In a strong leadership rhythm, you spend about 60 minutes of a 90-minute meeting doing IDS. That's where the real traction happens, and What–How–When supercharges that process. Here's how:

First, decide which issues deserve IDS time this week. You can't fix everything at once, so choosing what hits the table is the first act of prioritization. Second, as you work through IDS, apply the What–How–When lens. Identify what needs to be done, how to do it, and finally when to execute relative to the other issues in play.

This second prioritization is where timing decisions really get made. The When rarely happens in a vacuum. It's determined in comparison to every other initiative on the table. You weigh impact, resources, and bandwidth, asking yourself and your team questions, like the following:

- Which items make the biggest difference right now?
- Which items can be executed alongside each other?
- Which items are resource hogs that need to wait for a logical opening?

Combining IDS and What–How–When provides the structure, the logic, and the language to prioritize with precision. Together these two models turn weekly meetings from time-sinks into momentum machines.

"The Only Person Dumb Enough"

Years after the Actel whirlwind, I went to visit Scott Ross, the chairman of the board who had hired me for that impossible job with Trent Tetterton. Trent had been my direct boss and reported to Scott. By that time, Scott was retired and living in a mansion in Country Club of the South, a very posh area. I sat with Scott on his back porch with Trent, thanking them both for believing in me enough to hand me that VP of Sales and Marketing role at Actel.

"Scott, I really appreciate you picking me. You must have had a lot of great candidates, and you chose me."

He laughed, then he looked me dead in the eye and said, "Mel, you were the only one dumb enough to take that job. Everybody else told me no. But you almost pulled it off. I don't think anybody else could have."

I laughed. And in the years since then, I'd learned that what Scott said often ended up being true. Gunslingers are just "dumb" enough to believe that the impossible can become possible. It's what causes us to sign on to what looks like a losing battle—not because we think we're invincible, but because we believe we can build a team strong enough to fight through it. We've seen what people can do together when they're given the right leadership.

Building a Gunslinger Culture

A single gunslinger can save a business once. But the chances that the business will only deal with one problem, ever, is slim. If you want your business to last, you can't be the only one pulling the trigger. You need to build a culture where every department has gunslingers—leaders who move at the speed of business, act decisively, and course correct without fear. Overall, the top priority of being a gunslinger is protecting, fighting for and shepherding the culture. Let's talk about how to do it.

Push Decision-Making Down

The higher up you go, the more windows—opportunities— are opening and closing all over your business at any given moment. On your own, you can't possibly jump through all of them. You need to push the role of problem-solving closer to where it belongs so your department heads, managers, and even frontline teams have the clarity and authority to act.

Establish True-Ups

Don't make decisions that are supposed to last a month and then hope for the best. Build in weekly and quarterly *true-ups* or checkpoints. These true-ups keep the company on course and give everyone confidence that even if something goes wrong, you'll catch it fast and adjust.

Diagnose Dysfunction Early

Dysfunction doesn't age well. If a department is frozen, afraid to act, or constantly behind, that's a leadership problem. It could mean you've got an overbearing manager strangling the culture. Or it could mean you've got the wrong people in the wrong seats. Either way, fix it before it festers.

Protect the Culture

Every business has culture bandits—the rattlers and scorpions who slow things down, stir up politics, or undercut the vision. Gunslinger leaders don't waste time arguing with them. They remove them. Unite the team around one language, one vision, and one rhythm. That unity becomes your competitive advantage.

When you build a gunslinger culture, major shifts can occur. Employees stop hesitating because they know how to contribute and what's expected. Managers start leading boldly instead of through fear, and problems get solved fast before they turn into crises. Ultimately the whole organization begins to run like a well-oiled machine.

And outside the business's four walls, competitors start taking notice with a dose of healthy respect. Nobody wants to go toe-to-toe with a gunslinger company. They'd rather poach your people than try to beat you head-on. That's another problem for another chapter.

The mark of a true gunslinger culture is fear on the outside, confidence on the inside, and a team that can win at the speed of business.

The Gunslinger's Call

Business isn't won by being the fastest talker or having the fanciest strategies. It's won by the leaders who can act at the speed of business. Business is won when leaders see open windows, make the call, and get their people through safely before the opportunity is gone.

Business is won by the gunslingers—men and women who are decisive, fearless, tough, diagnostically smart, and committed to their people. The real goal isn't to be the lone hero riding from town to town forever. It's to build a team that can fight its own battles, a culture that runs without hesitation, and a business where dysfunction gets replaced with function at every level. Then and only then can you saddle up, move to the next frontier, and trust that the town you built will stand strong.

So here's your call to action:

- Start practicing What–How–When in every major decision.

- Build true-ups into your rhythm so course correction becomes second nature.
- Push decision-making down the line and give your people the confidence to act.
- And above all, run your company with a no-surprises culture. Trust and speed go hand in hand.

Do that, and you'll be more than a flash-in-the-pan fast draw. You'll be the kind of leader competitors fear, employees rally behind, and customers trust.

Now that you know how to build a problem-solving culture, we're going to bring part 2 to a close. It's time to move on to the next step—creating a Pony-Up culture.

Ready to ride? Let's go!

PART 3

Creating a Pony-Up Culture

Let's be honest. If things were going well, you wouldn't need this part of the book. And yet departments are feuding, trust is thin, and the whole place feels one bad day away from blowing up. You keep looking around and wondering who's going to fix it. The answer is *you* are. Part 3 gives you the tools, the posture, and the leadership edge to walk into the fire and come out with your team intact.

Chapter 10

The Leader Ponies Up First

There's a saying I've used for years with my teams, and it goes something like this:

You have to eat your own dog food.

If you're asking people to do something—if you want them to operate by a certain standard, follow a process, or embody a value—you'd better be doing it yourself first. In every business I've ever seen, the culture doesn't rise *above* the leader. It *follows* the leader.

And the leader needs to be the first one to *pony up*.

I learned this from my grandma when I was a young whippersnapper. No matter what we were doing, she'd always use "Because we take care of things" as her reason. That phrase was her way of reminding me that if something was worth doing, it was worth doing right, even when no one was looking.

I remember standing on a stool watching her make a pie when I was maybe 6 or 7. She carefully laid each blackberry into the crust, and I asked, "Why are you being so careful? Why can't you just dump it in there?"

"Because we take care of things, Mel," she'd say.

She'd say it again while she was fishing with us grandkids. She'd show us how to bait a hook so the worm wouldn't be easy for the fish to steal. But sometimes we got lazy about it. If the fish stole the bait, she'd shake her head and say with affectionate exasperation, "Mel, I showed you how to do this. You have to take care of things."

That lesson stuck with me.

Taking care of things is what leadership is all about. You don't get to skip the basics just because you're the boss. Show up on time, follow through, and keep your word. Say what you mean, and mean what you say. Make sure you're an example worth following; people can tell when a leader takes care of things. They *feel* it.

Your team should trust you. They should feel safe around you. And they should also have a healthy respect for you, knowing they can count on you to do what you said you'd do. They won't want to let you down.

As the leader of your business, you need to set the tone by being the first one to make good on your commitments and the first one to take responsibility. If things are going to get uncomfortable to move forward, you'll be the first in line.

A *pony-up culture* has to be modeled from the top. In this chapter, we'll talk about what that looks like in real life. Is it flashy? Not particularly. There's no magic button or software shortcut here. Real leaders earn the right to be followed by taking care of things every single day.

And nobody I ever met did that better than a man named Jim Stephens.

Jim was the son of the founder of the Elton B. Stephens Company (EBSCO). When I started working with them, it was a $4 billion company with 20 businesses and hundreds of brands under its umbrella. It was real big-time stuff, and he was a big-time leader. Most people were intimidated by him, but I wasn't. I was fascinated. Jim was the living, breathing example of what it looks like when a leader ponies up first.

Jim Stephens and the EBSCO Standard

EBSCO may be a digital titan when it comes to online research platforms and e-publications. But even back when I worked with them, they ran international operations on everything from magazines to digital distribution. It was massive, and although Jim Stephens had elevated out of running the business to be chairman of the board, he knew *every inch* of it.

Jim wasn't the kind of leader who led from a corner office or made appearances just to be seen. He was sharp as a tack, always well-dressed, and always on time. He carried himself with that quiet confidence of someone who didn't need to prove anything, and he didn't. He'd already done the work.

When Marshall Dillon walked into a room on the old Western television series *Gunsmoke*, people sat up straighter and took notice. Jim Stephens had that effect on an office too. When he walked through the door, people scrambled. They were nervous, because he knew exactly what was going on in every pocket of the company. He was liable to ask you some obscure question about a sub-brand in a subsidiary halfway around the world. Usually it was a question he already knew the answer to, and he was always right on target. You couldn't fake your way through a conversation with him.

Most people were intimidated, but I loved it when he showed up. It was a masterclass in true pony-up leadership.

He'd stroll into my office and say, "Hey Mel, have you seen this?" and plop down a report, pointing out a detail I'd never even heard of. Half the time, my answer was a sheepish, "Well, no I haven't seen that", and he'd nod, not angry, just expectant. I was always amazed at how aware he was of everything. He was running a company of thousands, yet he was so dialed into it that he'd find the *one* thing that mattered that week and bring it straight to your desk.

The thing that really made an impression on me though was the fact that he wasn't there to rub it in your face. He came because he genuinely *cared*.

If Jim Stephens pointed something out to you, he believed it mattered. He wanted to make a difference to the point that he was willing to ask the hard questions and expect answers. If he told you to look into something, you'd get a call or an email a week later asking, "Where are we on that?" He remembered, and he followed through.

Jim took care of things. He didn't only preach excellence—he lived it.

He could have thrown his title around or used fear to get results; he didn't. Instead, he led by example. Even though he was in his late seventies at the time, good luck keeping up with him. He had more energy, curiosity, and command than most people half his age, including me.

To this day, when I think of what it means to pony up as a leader, I think of Jim Stephens. He was the ultimate example of someone who didn't just hold other people accountable. He held himself accountable first, and he never asked others to do anything he wasn't already doing himself.

Jim had what I call mastery of the obvious. He focused on the simple, day-to-day things that make or break a business. These are the details most leaders overlook because they think they're above that kind of thing. But you know what? That kind of focus was what made him so powerful.

When you interacted with Jim, he left you sharper. You wanted to rise to the standard he set because you could see it lived out in him. That's the heart of pony- up leadership. If you're going to interact with people, make a difference by showing them what taking care of things actually looks like.

Ready to learn what that can look like for you and your business?

What It Means to Pony Up in Business

When I talk about pony-up leadership, I'm not talking about rolling up your sleeves once in a while and pretending you're one of the team for an "aw-shucks" photo op. I mean making good on your commitments, every single time.

Ponying up is a mindset and a way of leading that says, "If something's broken, it's my job to make sure it gets fixed, either by myself or the appropriate team member." It's a two-way street: Before you can expect your team to take ownership, *you* have to go first. If you're not taking care of the basics by showing up on time, keeping your promises, and making decisions quickly, then don't expect your people to.

A lot of businesses try to fix culture from the bottom up. They run engagement surveys, print new values on the wall, and hire consultants to "improve morale." But the truth is, culture doesn't start in HR. It starts with the leader taking a good, hard look in the mirror. If the leader doesn't pony up first, nothing sticks.

In every healthy organization I've worked with, the leaders do four things differently:

1. **Remove obstacles** that slow their people down.
2. **Create accountability systems** that keep progress visible and consistent.
3. **Live the discipline** they expect from everyone else.
4. **Provide crystal-clear expectations** so there's no confusion about what "good" looks like.

Although these four practices are simple, many leaders don't do them. They may *talk* about accountability, but they don't follow through. They *say* they want speed, but they bury decisions under layers of red tape. It's hard to know what pony-up leadership looks like since it's so seldom modeled well. So let's break down what these four practices look like, starting with the first responsibility of any true leader: removing obstacles.

Best Practice 1: Remove Obstacles

A leader's first job isn't to give speeches or make charts. It's to remove obstacles. Most of what keeps a business from growing isn't outside forces like the economy or the competition. The biggest obstacle that keeps a business from growing is the junk that's tolerated inside the business.

- Slow approvals
- Broken systems
- Meetings that go nowhere

A pony-up leader finds those obstacles and clears them out.

Think of it like this. If you were the leader of a wagon train and there was a boulder smack-dab in the middle of the trail, you'd find a way to move it, right? The journey is already difficult enough without having to reroute everyone to a different trail to avoid going to a little extra work rolling a stone away.

Business is already hard enough too. Between the competition, changing markets, and customer expectations, there's a lot to deal with every day that you have no control over. So for dad-gum sake, take care of the issues you *can*. Don't make your teams' jobs twice as hard by refusing to move the obstacles you can.

To help leaders think this way, I created a simple tool years ago. I call it the POCIT™ Tool (pronounced like "pocket").

P – Priorities

O – Obstacles

C – Control

I – Influence

T – Tasks

It's a simple exercise, and it changes how you think. When you use POCIT in your weekly meetings alongside IDS, it becomes a living system of obstacle removal. When you use it in your meetings, it looks like this:

Step 1: Determine the week's Priorities.

Step 2: Pinpoint any Obstacles standing in the way of those priorities being achieved.

Step 3: Identify who has Control over those obstacles and the power to remove them.

Step 4: Identify who has Influence over that person to get their buy-in.

Step 5: Assign Tasks that make the obstacle disappear.

Don't assign tasks and assume it'll get done. Follow up with a "Did you get it done?" the next time you meet. This creates accountability, greases the wheels of progress and creates massive momentum.

By being the pony-up leader that your business needs, you're steering things in the right direction. Don't come in and hype everyone up about vision and performance, then leave the team wrestling with broken tools, outdated software, and no authority to change anything. That's not inspiration. That's abandonment.

Whether they need a budget, permission to act, buy-in from another department, don't leave the meeting without clearing a path forward for your people to do their jobs. Removing obstacles isn't easy, but once they're gone, something powerful happens. People begin to trust the process. They see that when they bring up a problem, it gets solved. They stop wasting energy on workarounds and start putting that energy into results. The culture shifts from complaining to solving.

When your teams start to believe, "This is what we do here. We take care of things." *That's* when you know you're leading right.

Best Practice 2: Create Accountability Systems

Do you ever find that everybody starts off aligned after a big kickoff meeting, then six weeks later nobody knows what the priorities are? Your people are rowing hard but in different directions. It's frustrating, and you wonder why progress feels so dang slow. That's what drift looks like. When it comes to drift, the answer is simple. Accountability.

Once you've cleared the path, you've got to make sure people stay on it. That's where accountability comes in. You must create a consistent system that keeps everyone—yourself included—moving in the same direction week after week. Without an accountability system, you'll start to see drift.

The best way to infuse accountability into your business is through a weekly meeting cadence. We talked about the weekly meeting cadence in chapter 8. To quickly recap, you want a weekly meeting that's at the same time, on the same day, and at the same place every single week. During the meeting you start on time and follow a set agenda to help identify problems, prioritize goals, assign tasks, and provide accountability.

Discipline starts at the top. If you're loose, everyone else will be looser. I have sat in a lot of rooms where the one person blowing up the meeting was the leader. They'd stroll in ten minutes late, no agenda, open their laptop halfway through, then give a 40-minute speech about something no one can act on. And then they wonder why their people are unfocused. Don't do that.

If you want to go more in depth on a great system, I highly recommend the Entrepreneurial Operating System as outlined by Gino Wickman in his book, *Traction*. I'm not an EOS implementer; I'm a survivor of it. I've lived and breathed it by implementing it inside major corporations and organizations. I've been the one staying on the boat week after week, quarter after quarter, running the meetings, sticking to the discipline. There are many people who teach it. I've *done* it.

If you want to dig deeper into how to structure accountability meetings or build a rhythm your team can rely on, there are more resources on my website. But when it comes to accountability, there's one really important thing to remember.

Accountability is *not* micromanagement. It's *rhythm*. It's clarity plus consistency.

When everyone knows that the team meets, follows up, and does what it says it will do, they'll do their part. If someone misses a to-do, the response isn't panic or excuses. It's "Okay, it's on the board; we'll fix it." There's no room for drama, blame, or hiding—just truth.

Accountability is vital, and a good pony-up leader needs something else too. They need to be disciplined.

Best Practice 3: Be Disciplined

Accountability without discipline is just paperwork. What do I mean by that? Well you can run all the meetings you want, and if you're not living by the same rules you're handing out, it's all talk.

I've seen too many companies with slick core values painted on the wall in fancy fonts, while the leaders behind them don't live up to a single one. They'll say things like "We value honesty" right before they dodge a hard conversation or "We value teamwork" right before they throw someone under the bus. People notice that.

You can't uphold core values if you don't live up to them. So if you can't live up to them, change them. Or better yet, clean up your act and live them. Your business culture will always take its cues from you. If you say you want a culture that shows up on time, then you show up on time. If you say, "no phones in meetings," then put your phone away. If you say, "structure first, people second," then stick to the agenda instead of giving a 40-minute tangent about your weekend.

It's simple stuff. It's also the difference between a business that hums along in momentum and one that grinds and bumps along in stop-and-go mode.

Discipline is doing what you said you'd do, especially when you don't feel like it.

Sometimes discipline means doing the hard thing, like when granddad goes out to shoot the old horse. Nobody *wants* to do it, but if you don't, the whole farm suffers. That's leadership. When there's something tough that has to be done, you don't hand it off. *You* do it first.

The same thing goes in a business. If you've got rattlesnakes or culture bandits who are poisoning your business, spreading negativity, and creating chaos—it's *your* job to get rid of them. Don't leave it to HR or an outside consultant. We'll talk more about dealing with culture bandits in chapter 12. Just know that if you won't deal with them, nobody else will.

I can't tell you how many times I've walked into a business and found the person who hired me sitting at a table full of rattlesnakes. When I tell them it's time to start firing, they say, "Mel, I can't get rid of them—this is my whole team."

And I'll tell them, "Well, you should've fixed it a long time ago."

If you truly care about your people, you'll protect them from mediocrity and dysfunction. You'll remove the things—and the people—that keep everyone else from doing their best work. Discipline isn't cruel. It's care with consequences.

You don't have to be the loudest or the meanest person in the room. But you do have to be the most *consistent.* Be one who does what they say, even when it's hard, even when it's unpopular, and even when it hurts a little. Leadership isn't about comfort. Without discipline, you'll lose credibility. And that's one thing you never want to lose.

Now let's talk about the fourth practice of pony-up leadership—providing clarity.

Best Practice 4: Provide Clarity

Even the best people can't perform in the dark. If you want your team to pony up, they've got to know what they're aiming at and how fast they're supposed to get there. That means you need to set the standard for clarity, and it begins by defining your peoples' *span of control.*

Let's say you're the ranch foreman out on the range, driving the cowherd to market. You and your team of cowhands are responsible for 1,000 head of cattle, and it's your job to get them from point A to point B in a safe and timely manner. Would you ride out on your own and try to do it all yourself? Would you turn your cowhands loose without a plan?

Heck no! You'd die trying to do it on your own, and it would be a disaster to send your cowhands out on the range without clear instructions. You'd lay it all out for them, split them up into pairs responsible for a portion of the herd, and divide responsibilities among everyone. Each cowhand would then be able to confidently ride out knowing exactly what to do, how to do it, and when they were expected to do it.

You'd have your span of control, and they'd have theirs.

The span of control is the range of responsibility a leader can realistically manage without slowing things down. If you're trying to lead too many people or too big a territory, you're carrying too much. Your team won't be able to move at the speed of business because you've overloaded the system.

Start by tightening the span of control. Simplify who reports to whom, make sure roles make sense, and give people the power they actually need to do their jobs. If someone has to run every small decision up the ladder for approval, you've already lost speed.

And your responsibility? You need to be freed up to be able to act and react at the speed of business.

If it takes two days to sign off on something you could've approved in one, you doubled the cost of that decision. You killed momentum. When momentum dies, culture follows right behind it.

Questions to Ponder

Not sure where you're sitting in terms of clarity right now? Ask yourself:

- Do my people have what they need to make decisions quickly?
- Do they know what "good" looks like?
- Do our structures enable or restrict progress?

When you answer those questions honestly, you'll be able to identify the friction points that are holding you back and costing you momentum. These friction points are where most businesses lose their energy.

Before we move on, let's talk about a few important areas where clarity is the hero that saves the day.

Intra-department vs. Inter-department Clarity

Part of clarity in your business is knowing the difference between intra- and inter-department dynamics and handling them well.

- **Intra-department** is what happens inside a single team—their meetings, tasks, and workflows. Intra-department concerns should be handled by the individual head of each team.

- **Inter-department** is what happens between teams—sales to operations, operations to service, and service to finance. These issues need to be addressed by you.

Most of the big problems in a business live in the *inter* space where departments collide, duplicate effort, or blame each other.

A pony-up leader doesn't sit and watch inter-department conflict happen. They step in. They grab the departments that are butting heads, put them at the same table, and say, "Let's figure this out." Then they stay there until the problem's solved.

When leaders don't do that, teams start building walls instead of bridges. Once that happens, accountability breaks down across the whole business.

Clarity in Compensation

Clarity in a pony-up culture also extends to compensation. Some leaders say they want teamwork; they then pay people to hoard credit. They'll say they want profitability; then they compensate only for top-line revenue. They'll say they want customer satisfaction; then they never tie compensation to it.

Then they wonder why their people aren't producing the results they want. The answer is simple. You get what you pay for.

If people are confused about how they get paid, or worse, if they're being paid to do things that hurt the business, you've got a structural problem. It's not a personnel problem.

The solution is to pay people for the job you *want* them to do.

I can't tell you how many businesses I've seen that accidentally pay people to do the opposite of what they say they want. Then they spend months in meetings trying to "fix morale" or "drive accountability," when the real problem is right there in the compensation plan.

If you ever say, "You get paid when we get paid," and someone threatens to quit—good. You found a broken piece of your business. What they're really thinking is, *I don't trust the system to deliver on its end.* That's gold for a leader. That's where you dig in and find out what's broken.

Don't stop at the symptom. Go fix the root cause.

If your compensation plans encourage behavior that goes against your goals, fix them. If another department controls something that affects your people's compensation, that's a problem. Because people won't stay engaged when their paycheck depends on something they can't control. Don't let another department's structure create a roadblock for your people. Don't make them chase metrics that pull against each other.

I've had people tell me, "Mel, that's just how our structure works."

And I'll tell them, "Then fix your structure."

That's what a pony-up leader does. They don't throw the problem back on the team and say, "Y'all need to figure that out." They sit down with them, dig into the incentives, and make sure people are rewarded for the behaviors that actually move the business forward.

And it's not just about money. Rewards can be recognition, responsibility, or growth opportunities. You can run contests, highlight wins, celebrate interdepartmental success—anything that reinforces the behaviors you want more of.

Let me give you a funny example of accidentally reinforcing behavior the *wrong* way from the marketing world. In 1976, Michelob launched a new slogan. "Weekends Were Made for Michelob." You can guess what happened. They had massive sales spikes on the weekend and dead sales Monday through Thursday. The company got exactly what they asked for, but not what they needed.

By the early 80s, they'd decided to double down with a new slogan: "Michelob Light for the Winners." It was wildly successful. People drank Michelob Light when they were celebrating. The problem was that sales spiked after big events, then plummeted the rest of the time.

That's how incentives work. If you're not careful, you'll create short bursts of activity that look like success but actually starve your business long-term. A pony-up leader doesn't chase spikes; they build systems that sustain.

A pony-up leader looks at the system as a whole and makes sure it all connects from structure to roles, meetings, incentives, and communication. When everyone knows exactly what's expected and has the authority and motivation to deliver, you get alignment. And alignment is where excellence lives.

From Ponying Up to Placing People Right

When you start leading from the front and pony up first, something interesting happens. You stop tolerating excuses. You stop overlooking broken systems. And eventually, you stop lying to yourself about the real problem.

Once you've taken care of your end—your structure, your discipline, your accountability—you'll start to see where the real friction in the business lives. Most of the time, it's not the process. It's the people.

This is where most leaders get tripped up. They'll see someone struggling and think, "Well, maybe I need to teach or coach them better." But sometimes that leader is trying to teach a cat to bark.

In the next chapter, I'll show you how to recognize whether you're trying to teach a cat to bark. I'll teach you why it happens and what to do when the person you've got isn't the person for the seat. Ponying up doesn't stop at doing your job well. It means having the guts to face the truth about who's sitting in which seat and making the call no one else will make.

Asking a Cat to Bark

I was sitting in a leadership meeting one morning, listening to a group of managers argue about why a certain department wasn't hitting their numbers. After about five minutes of pointing fingers and back-and-forth, I leaned back, looked around the table and said, "Whoa, whoa, whoa now. Here's your problem: You're asking a cat to bark."

The room went quiet. Then somebody laughed, and the whole room cut up.

I know asking a cat to bark sounds like a funny joke. But it's not, and I wasn't laughing.

"I wouldn't do that, Mel," said one of the managers. "That doesn't make any sense."

Of course it didn't make sense, and yet it happens all the time in a lot of businesses. When you take a good employee and put them in the wrong seat, that's as nonsensical as asking a cat to bark. Then to get frustrated when that person couldn't—or wouldn't—do what the managers want? Well that makes even less sense, if you asked me.

"He'll get it eventually," another manager chimed in. "He's such a great guy, and he's doing an okay job. I'm sure once he sees how important this role is to the company, he'll step up."

Except I knew he wouldn't. He *couldn't* because it wasn't in him. They were asking a cat to bark. The longer they kept at it, the more they taught their whole organization to accept mediocrity as normal.

Looking around the boardroom that day, I could tell the moment the meaning of asking a cat to bark sank in. The laughter in the boardroom tapered off, and the managers grew serious. They knew exactly what I was talking about, and they knew they'd been guilty of doing it. We all have. But until you stop pretending your cat is a dog, your business will not run right.

The Truth About Misalignment

Remember back in chapter 7 when we talked about structure first, people second? Well this chapter is what tends to happen *after* that when you realize somebody you care about doesn't belong in the fort you built.

Sooner or later, you're going to look around and see that an employee is not thriving in their position. They might be a great person—loyal, hard-working, and kind. Heck, they might even be a family member. But if the seat calls for a dog and you've put a cat in it, no amount of pep talks or training programs will change the fact that your business has a misalignment.

The person isn't a good fit, and that's okay. Admitting it doesn't mean you're judging their worth. You're acknowledging their wiring. The hard part is, most leaders don't want to admit it. We'd rather spend months convincing ourselves it's a "development opportunity" or that "they need more coaching."

That right there is denial, plain and simple. You know the truth, and you're afraid of the fallout that comes with facing it.

I get it. I've been there. It may seem easier to keep pretending for a little while longer. But that little while can turn into too long faster than you think. Misalignment doesn't fix itself—it compounds. The longer you let it ride, the more it's going to cost you.

Here's what happens when you ignore a misalignment:

- Other team members start tiptoeing around the problem.
- Meetings turn into therapy sessions.
- Accountability gets blurry because everyone's afraid to step on toes.
- Eventually good people leave because the culture tells them results don't matter.

Ouch. Those aren't results you want inside your business. So what do you do? Well I'll tell you what you *don't* have to do. You don't have to rebuild your whole structure to fix this. You have to tell the truth about who fits where.

The right person in the wrong seat will burn out and lose confidence.

The wrong person in the right seat will burn *you* out.

Either way, it's your job to fix it.

Leadership isn't about being nice. It's about helping maintain alignment between the role and the person. The moment you correct a misalignment, you'll feel it. The business breathes easier. Communication clears up, and energy comes back.

So before you try to motivate, train, or coach someone who's not performing, stop and ask yourself if what you're really doing is asking a cat to bark. If the answer is yes, you have a decision to make.

But before we dive into what to do, let's talk about why this happens.

Why Leaders Keep Asking Cats to Bark

If you've led people for any length of time, you've done it. You see potential in someone you like within the company. They've been loyal, they're easy to get along with, and you really like them as a person. Maybe they've been with the company since the beginning, making sacrifices and staying committed even in the face of obstacles. So when they start struggling in their role in the business, your first instinct isn't to question the fit. Your first instinct is to jump in and help.

You think, *If I can just pour into them a little more, they'll get it.*

That's noble, but it's wrong. You're trying to save them from a seat they were never meant to fill. Every time you do that, you send a message to your whole team that outcomes are negotiable if you're nice enough.

Let me tell you, nothing wrecks momentum faster than that. I've watched whole businesses slow to a crawl because a leader couldn't bring themselves to have one hard conversation. They'll spend six months designing "improvement plans," six more months moving the person sideways into another department, and then another year trying to convince themselves that it's working. By then, good people are frustrated, the culture's sideways, and the leader's credibility has taken a hit.

I once had a department head who was a fantastic operator but couldn't lead people to save his life. I thought I could fix it by staying close. We had extra meetings together, and I gave him extra coaching, training, pep talks—the whole works. In the end, all I did was build a dependency. He leaned harder on me, his team got more confused, and I got busier doing a job that wasn't mine.

I was *helping* him fail slower.

When I finally made the call to move him out of leadership and back into an operational role, it was like the whole company exhaled. He was relieved too. He didn't want the seat anymore. I was the only one still pretending he did. I was so close to the situation that I didn't realize I'd been asking a cat to bark. Since then, I've learned that there are signs when you're asking a cat to bark.

Signs You're Asking a Cat to Bark

Not sure how to tell if you've been asking a cat to bark? Here are some fast, practical indicators that can clue you in:

- They work hard and are well-liked but don't get the outcomes the position requires.
- You find yourself making exceptions so they can "win" such as custom targets, extended deadlines, or special handling.
- You or other team members often end up doing their job.
- Cross-team friction at the handoffs where this role should create flow.
- You're personally jumping in to unclog issues this role should own.

You may think you're being merciful in giving this person more chances, but really, you're avoiding the truth. Avoidance always costs more than honesty. You don't fix misalignment by being nicer or doing their job. You fix it by facing the truth, getting clear on what's really going on, and dealing with it. The longer you delay, the harder it will be to fix the misalignment. The cost of lying to yourself could become too high a price to pay.

The Cost of Lying to Yourself

Every time you tell yourself *it'll work itself out*, you're trading short-term comfort for long-term cancer. When you refuse to see and deal with a misalignment, you're teaching your team that the standard doesn't matter. You're telling them that results are optional as long as you've been around long enough or mean well enough.

That's how mediocrity takes root. Mediocrity can sneak in disguised as loyalty and patience. *Awww, I'll just give them one more chance.* But what about everyone else? Before you know it, your best people are quietly disengaging when they see what you're pretending not to.

Your team always knows before you admit it. They know who's not pulling their weight and who's out of their depth. And they're watching to see how long you'll tolerate it. Once they realize you're willing to lie to yourself about it, they start lying to you too. When that happens, you not only lose performance. You lose trust, and trust is the only real currency you have as a leader.

I've walked into plenty of companies where the CEO was hoping things would turn around. They had good systems, clear goals, and decent people. Yet the air in the place was heavy. You could feel it. That's what structural dishonesty feels like. It hangs over every meeting like a fog. Once that fog settles in, momentum dies.

Nobody moves fast in an environment where truth is optional. You can put a thousand motivational posters on the wall, but if everyone knows there's a sacred cow nobody's allowed to talk about, that's the only message that matters.

When you tolerate misalignment, you may tell yourself you're protecting someone. You're actually poisoning the well. You're telling every hard-working person in your business that effort doesn't matter as much as emotion.

I hate to break it to you, but that's how you lose your A-players. They don't leave for money. They leave because they no longer feel like what they're doing matters.

So if you feel like your team has lost its spark or your meetings feel like quicksand, check how honest you're being with yourself before checking anything else. The truth can fix what denial keeps breaking if you let it.

Leadership isn't about comfort. Leadership is about championing clarity. And yes, clarity can feel like conflict at first. But things can only get back on track when you stop pretending the cat's ever going to start acting like a dog and deal with it.

Now let's talk about how to deal with it and how to prevent misalignment from happening in the first place.

The Right-Seat Decision Framework

Once you've told yourself the truth, you've got three choices:

- Move them
- Part ways
- Rebuild the seat

I'm not trying to be cold-hearted here, but anything else is avoidance dressed up as strategy. If you've got the wrong person in the wrong seat, you're both losing. It's your job to put every person where they can actually *win*.

Here's how I decide whether to move them, fire them, or rebuild a seat:

1. If you have a great person in the wrong seat, move them.

If they're just not wired for this particular role but they fit your culture, share your values, and genuinely care about the mission, find them a better fit if you can.

Let's say you've got a loyal, detail-oriented team member leading a high-speed sales function...and it's not going well. Their deliberateness is throwing a wrench in the nonstop cadence of sales. They're not lazy. They're simply not wired to live in chaos. You're asking a cat to bark. Stop and move them to a role where their precision is a superpower instead of a liability.

Moving someone is only an effective strategy if the seat *actually exists*. Don't invent one to make yourself feel better. Creating fake roles is how businesses turn into refugee camps for misplaced talent.

What to say:

> "You're a strong player, and you've brought a lot of value here. But the role you're in right now doesn't match what you're best at, and that's not fair to you or the team.
>
> I've spent some time looking at where your natural strengths actually shine, and I think we can align you better. That doesn't mean you've failed. It means this seat isn't the right one. Let's talk about where you can have the most impact and what that transition might look like."

2. If you have the wrong person in the right seat, part ways. If the seat is clear and the expectations are clear, but the person still doesn't get it, want it, or have the capacity to do it, they don't fit in that seat. It's time to cut ties.

When I'm evaluating whether or not someone is the wrong person in the right seat, I use the EOS concept of Get It, Want It, Capacity (GWC). I ask myself:

> **Get It:** Do they understand the role and what success looks like?
>
> **Want It:** Do they actually *want* to do it, or are they just collecting a paycheck?
>
> **Capacity:** Do they have the time, skill, and emotional bandwidth to handle it?

If any of those are a "no," let them go. Period. Cutting ties quickly and respectfully protects both of you. They get the dignity of clarity, and you get your momentum back.

What to say:

> "I need to have a straight conversation with you. The expectations for this seat have been clear for a while now, and we haven't seen consistent progress toward them.
>
> This isn't about effort. You've worked hard. But the role requires certain results, and at this point, it's clear this isn't the right fit.
>
> I'm grateful for what you've contributed, and I want to make sure we end this well and help you land in a place where your strengths can actually win."

3. If it's the wrong person in the wrong seat, rebuild the seat and start over.

Sometimes the problem isn't the person *or* the performance. Sometimes it's the seat itself. Maybe the role was designed too vaguely, or you've let it morph into a Frankenstein job that nobody could succeed in. If you look at the seat and can't define its purpose, outcomes, and authority in one sentence each, that's on you as the leader. It's time to tear the seat down and rebuild it clean.

Once the seat makes sense again, *then* look for the right person.

These decisions are never fun, but they're necessary for the health of your business and the rest of your employees. Don't let loyalty, fear, guilt, or pride keep you from doing the right thing. The real job of leadership is to face the truth faster than everyone else and act on it. Doing that will help you spot misalignment quickly and deal with it appropriately.

When you start dealing with these issues, there's bound to be talk. People will have questions, and you want to make sure you're in control of the story.

What to say:

> "You've probably noticed a few changes lately. We've been tightening up our structure to make sure everyone's in the right seat and doing the work they're best at.
>
> That's not about playing favorites. It's about alignment and clarity.
>
> You can expect more of this kind of change in the months ahead, because that's how healthy organizations grow. We don't hide from the truth. We use it to get better."

When you start moving people around, the whole system wobbles for a bit. That's normal. Here's how to deal with it in a way that helps the company come out stronger.

Holding the Line

You can't reshuffle key seats and expect everything to run like a well-oiled machine right away. The gears are realigning, and somebody has to make sure they don't grind. Guess what? *You* are the one who needs to hold the line. It's the leader's job to stabilize the new structure so it doesn't rattle apart during transition periods. Change doesn't have to equal chaos.

Once the gears mesh and start turning smoothly again, you step back quietly. No need for parades or speeches. After all that, you won't need one anyway. The steady hum where there used to be noise will be all the music your ears need.

Mercy and Math

Leadership is a blend of mercy and math. Mercy is about people, and math is about performance. If you get those two out of balance, your business starts to wobble.

If you lean too hard on mercy, you'll keep people in seats they can't handle because you feel sorry for them. You'll spend your days managing emotions instead of results. But if you lean too hard on math, you'll treat people like numbers, and pretty soon your culture will go cold.

So what do you do? You strive to keep mercy and math in tension, so you can lead with both head *and* heart.

Real leadership isn't easy. Sometimes it means having to look someone in the eye and say, "I care about you, and that's exactly why I can't let this continue." If you want a business that scales without losing its soul, this is the line you walk.

Every cat you move, every misalignment you fix, and every honest conversation you have reinforces one truth: The health of your business depends on your willingness to stay honest.

So don't lie to yourself. Don't build workarounds for people who aren't built for the work, and don't confuse being nice with being kind.

Mercy gives people a fair shot, but math keeps the business alive. Surprise, surprise—you need both.

When you get mercy and math working together, something powerful happens. Clarity begins to replace chaos, performance replaces politics, and everyone in the business starts breathing a little easier.

That's what happens when you stop asking cats to bark.

Now misalignment is one thing—it's usually innocent. Good people in the wrong seats. Wrong wiring, right intentions. But there's another kind of problem that runs deeper. Every once in a while, you'll find someone who's not only in the wrong seat; they're actively poisoning the well.

This type of person resists every improvement, stirs up drama, and slows down the people who are trying to move forward. When you see a person like that, you're not looking at a case of asking cats to bark. You're looking at a culture bandit.

And dealing with culture bandits requires a different kind of conversation altogether.

Chapter 12

Dealing With Culture Bandits

If you walk into your baby's room and there's a rattlesnake coiled in the crib, you don't form a committee. You don't call HR. You don't send an email to "circle back."

You act.

You get the baby to safety and grab the nearest shovel. You don't leave that room until the danger is gone because that's what a parent does when something threatens what they love.

That's what a business leader does for their culture.

Your business culture is the living, breathing thing, and you're responsible for protecting it. That rattlesnake you're facing is a type of person I call a culture bandit. This person makes fatal, countercultural choices and decides they're above the mission. They don't just break rules. They break trust. And the longer they stay, the more people they bite.

When it comes to culture bandits, the mistake most leaders make is debating whether the snake *means* to be a snake. They start asking questions like:

"Well, what if they're just misunderstood?"
"What if they're too valuable to lose?"
"Can't we retrain them?"

Meanwhile, the baby's still in the crib.

A right-thinking leader doesn't stand around and debate. He *acts*. Seeing the danger and failing to act means you've already chosen sides, and it's not the side you want to be on.

After all, your job isn't to protect the rattler. Your job is to protect the baby.

Being a leader requires the courage to see clearly and act decisively when culture is under threat. In this chapter, I'm going to show you how to recognize and deal with culture bandits. Once you learn to recognize a culture bandit, you'll stop wasting time arguing about whether they can change and start leading like someone who actually knows what's at stake. So...what makes someone a culture bandit?

Who is a Culture Bandit?

Not every problem person is a rattlesnake. Sometimes you've got a cat in a dog role. When that happens, the person isn't trying to cause trouble. They're not trying to sabotage the company, but they're not in the right seat.

A culture bandit is something else entirely.

A culture bandit is a person who's decided—consciously or not—that the mission, values, and momentum of the business don't apply to them. They create their own little country inside your company where they build resistance and manipulate the narrative. And they're usually talented enough to fool people for a while.

Culture bandits not only slow you down. They redirect momentum. They'll pit departments against each other, twist words in meetings, and spread half-truths that sound plausible enough to plant seeds of doubt and discord. An Old West bandit may walk into a saloon with guns blazing, but culture bandits don't need to do that. A subtle eye roll in a meeting can cause enough internal tension to derail the entire thing.

So how do you spot a culture bandit before they bite? I recommend using my Feel-Hear-See Framework.

The Feel–Hear–See Framework

Every leader unconsciously operates on three levels of understanding—feeling, hearing, and seeing. The faster you learn to consciously move up that ladder, the wiser and more decisive you become.

Step 1: Feel

Feel is the first level of understanding, and this is where most people stop. They end up leading from emotion and how they feel about things. The problem with that is feelings are changeable and not always based on fact. They can be hijacked by gossip, mood, or the loudest voice in the room. A culture bandit only needs a few emotionally-driven people to swing the whole crowd off course.

Feelings matter, but they're low validity. It's important to quickly move to the next rung on the ladder.

Step 2: Hear

Hear is the next step up. You're paying attention to what's being said in meetings, emails, and hallway conversations and listening for alignment or distortion. That's important to do; yet words can still be twisted. A culture bandit can say all the right things and mean none of them. Although hearing gives you more data than feelings, it's still filtered through opinion, tone, and ego.

That's why it's important to keep moving to the final level of understanding.

Step 3: See

The final level of understanding is See. When you see, you're observing something with your own eyes over time, without spin. Seeing helps you understand behavior in action and what people actually *do* when no one's watching.

Real trust is built in seeing. After all, you can trust people to do what you've already seen them do. I'm a strong believer in that statement, and you can take it to the bank too.

If someone has shown loyalty, consistency, and care for the mission, you can trust that. If they've shown deceit, drama, or contempt, you can trust that too. People generally continue to do what you've seen them do in the past.

Your job as a leader is to keep climbing the Feel–Hear–See ladder. Start by acknowledging what you Feel, then verify it by what you Hear. But make decisions based on what you See.

Putting Feel–Hear–See into Action

Feel–Hear–See isn't just something you know about. You *use* it. Think of it like a communication triangle that keeps your team aligned when the pressure's on.

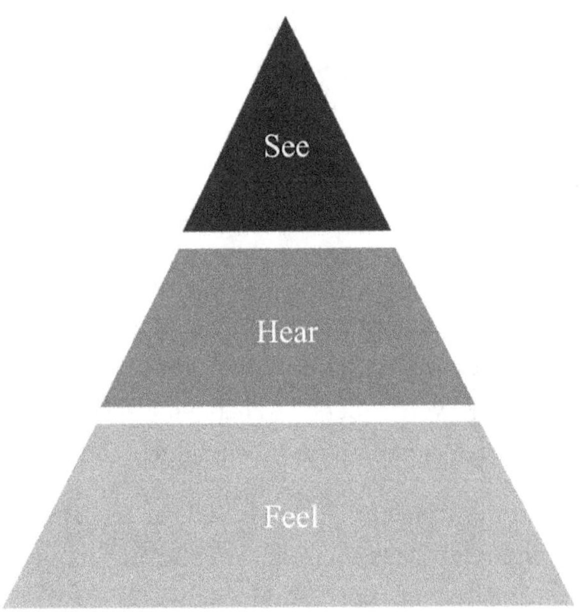

At the bottom is Feel. This is the foundation of every culture. You want people who feel the same way about work, integrity, and mission that you do. That's how you find your coachable people. They're the folks who get excited about the vision and don't roll their eyes at hard work or accountability.

Hiring and developing through shared feeling isn't soft; it's smart. If people don't feel right about your values, they'll never fully align with them.

In the middle is Hear. Once you've got people with shared feelings, the next step is helping them hear the same message clearly, repeatedly, and in language they can understand. It's at the Hear level that most businesses lose unity. The Tower of Babel wasn't destroyed by lack of effort. It was destroyed by confusion of language.

Your job as a leader is to make sure your people hear the same thing the same way. That means slowing down, clarifying what matters, and repeating it until it sticks. I recommend communicating seven times in seven ways. Utilize meetings, one-on-ones, scorecards, dashboards, videos, emails, company updates—whatever it takes to clearly get the message across so it's heard and understood the same way by everyone.

At the top of the triangle is See. This is where understanding turns into wisdom. People have to see what success looks like. That's why visuals like org charts, dashboards, and KPIs matter. A quick glance should tell anyone how they're doing and how their work connects to the whole.

When people can *see* progress, they believe in it. When they can see the truth in the numbers, in the behavior, and in their leader's example, they'll trust it. And when they trust what they see, the culture becomes self-reinforcing.

The goal of Feel–Hear–See is this:

- Feel: Align hearts
- Hear: Unify language
- See: Reinforce truth through evidence

When you move people through that progression, you create shared vision, shared language, and shared accountability. Confusion is eliminated, and you're able to build trust, and accelerate momentum all without yelling, begging, or micromanaging.

Those who aren't a good fit will become more noticeable. And you know who else is now easily identifiable? Culture bandits. When you see a culture bandit, you'll know what to do. The next move may not be easy, but it isn't complicated. Before we dive into that, let me give you an example of Feel–Hear–See in action.

Case Study: The Holding Company That Lost Its Sight

A few years back, a multibillion-dollar holding company brought me in to figure out why one of their subsidiaries was tanking. On paper, it looked like a sales problem. Revenue was down and morale was low. The board assumed the salespeople weren't doing their jobs and had gotten lazy.

I walked in expecting to rebuild a sales department. It took me less than 24 hours to realize they were dealing with something entirely different. The salespeople weren't the problem. Surprisingly, it was the leadership team.

When the original president of the subsidiary company had retired, the holding company brought in an entirely new set of executives. These executives were smart people with very polished resumes. On the surface it looked like they were doing well. They had all the buzzwords down and said they were working to "restructure" the business and "reimagine" its future. Yet internally, the business was falling apart.

When I looked a little closer, I discovered that behind the scenes, the new leaders loathed the very brands they were supposed to champion. They were mistreating long-time employees, cutting off communication between teams, and sabotaging the old guard so they could look like saviors when everything broke.

I sat with them privately, and the level of arrogance and contempt was shocking. They didn't even try to hide it. They openly mocked the legacy teams and belittled the people who had built those brands and carried them through decades of success.

Remember the Feel–Hear–See hierarchy?

At first, I *felt* sympathy for the new team. They seemed frustrated, and that can be hard to deal with.

Then I *heard* their stories and their complaints. They were pretty dang convincing, and it sounded like they had valid concerns

But when I *saw* the operation, my perception of what was going on flipped. The sales teams weren't broken. They were really good at what they did. But they were suffocating under bad leadership. The real problem was sitting around the executive table.

The danger of blindness at the top is when you can't—or won't—see clearly, and your business becomes hostage to people who don't deserve to lead it. This instance was living proof, and fixing it wasn't going to be easy.

Initially the holding company board members didn't want to believe me. After all they'd hired these executives, and they were convinced this new team was brilliant. And maybe they were, but they weren't aligned with the vision and language of the company. Brilliance without alignment is poison.

I had to break the cold, hard truth to them. I told them their subsidiaries had been hijacked by culture bandits, and it was time to deal with it.

It took a year to unwind the mess and clean up the business's culture. We had to remove the entire leadership team, rebuild the structure, and restore trust from the ground up. Was it painful? Oh yes. But the moment those rattlers were no longer in the crib with the baby, the whole organization could breathe again. Momentum came back, people pulled together, and the culture began to heal.

If you're dealing with needing a culture clean up, your role as a leader is vital. How do you lead through culture cleansing without everything falling apart?

How to Lead Through Culture Cleansing

Dealing with culture bandits isn't only about swinging the shovel and throwing the rattlers out. It's also about protecting momentum while you do it.

Momentum is the invisible force that makes an organization hum. It's the reason meetings feel sharp, people stay late, and problems get solved before you even knew they existed. When momentum dies, good people start checking out. They may smile, but they stop speaking up. Culture bandits thrive in that silence.

Once the culture bandits are out of there, you'll have some rebuilding to do to repair the damage these rattlesnakes did on the inside. If you want to rebuild a healthy culture, you'll want to start at the top with the senior team. That's where the vision lives, and that's where the damage will lead to decay if you don't deal with it. Here's how to begin the healing process:

Get on the Same Page

The top leaders will all need to get on the same page. You can't fix what you don't agree on. Depending on how much damage was done, that won't happen automatically. You'll have to work through whatever conflicts or misunderstandings popped up through meetings and open conversations.

Set the Standard

While you're meeting to get on the same page, sit down together and define the vision, core values, and the quarterly and annual goals. Write it all down. If you use EOS, pull out the Vision Traction Organizer. If you don't, grab a whiteboard and a dry erase marker. Either way, clarity at the top creates traction everywhere else.

Cascade the Message

Once you've got the visions, values, and goals down, it's time to start spreading the message down the line. Have the top leaders carry the message to their teams through multiple channels. Telling people once is not enough. I like to say that the best way to make sure vision, values, and goals sticks is to share it seven times in seven ways. Don't just say it once in a meeting. Say it repeatedly in meetings, emails, calls, one-on-ones, company literature—you name it. You're not overcommunicating. You're taking out insurance against the spread of distorted information.

Watch for Smoke

Once the shared vision, values, and goal have been shared, watch for smoke. Things won't automatically improve because your communication has become more effective. Down in the business, you'll see where things start to bog down. It might be people, process, or communication. It might be altered language or missing data or a manager "forgetting" to cascade the message. When you see the smoke, follow it.

Trust What You See

When you find the source of the smoke, don't hesitate. If it's a system issue, fix it. If it's a people issue, address it. And if it's a culture bandit who's actively undermining the mission, separate them from the business quickly, cleanly, and respectfully. You're not being cruel. You're being responsible.

In fact, don't be afraid to pay them to leave. If it costs six months' pay to get the snake out of the crib, pay it. You can replace the money, and the sooner you take care of it, the sooner your business will bounce back.

Nothing rallies a team faster than seeing a leader protect them. When you act decisively, your people will see it. They'll pull tighter together, even if it means extra work for a while. Culture changes through action. When people know their leader will guard the baby, they'll guard it too.

As a leader, you'll need that kind of decisive action for sure. But you'll also need something else that we alluded to earlier. You're going to need wisdom and discernment. Let me tell you an old fable that will illustrate what I mean.

The Scorpion and the Frog Revisited

There once was a valley where a frog and a scorpion lived. One day a flood swept through the valley. The water began to rise dangerously. The scorpion saw a young frog swimming to safety and, desperate not to drown, begged for his help.

"Please," he cried, "let me ride on your back so I can get to safety. If you don't help me, I'll die."

The frog hesitated. "You're a scorpion. You sting things, and if you stung me, I'd die. Why would I let you ride with me?"

"Think about it," the scorpion pleaded. "If I sting you, we'll both drown. Why would I do that?"

It made sense. The frog felt sorry for him, so he let the scorpion climb onto his back and resumed swimming to safety. Halfway across, the scorpion struck. As the venom spread and they both began to sink, the frog gasped, "Why would you do that? Now we'll both die."

The scorpion answered, "Because it's in my nature."

That's how human nature operates in business too. Some people will just keep stinging, even if it means they'll go down with you. You can't change their nature, and it's not your job to try. Your job is to recognize it. And that's where wisdom comes in. Wisdom is what happens when you've moved beyond feelings and words into sight and discernment. It's knowing what's in front of you and acting in a way that protects the whole, not just the parts.

In this way, trust is a power word. Trust doesn't mean giving people the benefit of the doubt repeatedly when they've proven they haven't earned it. It means relying on the evidence of what you've seen.

If someone consistently acts with integrity, you can trust them to keep doing it. If someone lies, manipulates, or divides, you can recognize the patterns and trust them to act accordingly.

When you build a culture around this kind of clear-eyed trust, your people thrive because they don't have to guess what's real. They know their leader sees, hears, and acts based on truth.

And let's not forget about the other side of the fable. The frog wasn't wrong to be kind, but he was foolish to ignore the evidence. In leadership, compassion without boundaries is cruelty in disguise. You can't put good people in the path of those who will harm them and call it grace. A good shepherd doesn't let wolves roam among the sheep just to see if they'll behave this time.

If you can't see, you can't lead. If you see but refuse to act, you become an accomplice instead of a shepherd. Wisdom is seeing clearly, trusting what you've seen, and having the courage to act on it no matter how uncomfortable it feels. It's only after you *act* that your business can become a safe place again

A Safe Town at Last

There's a moment after a long gunfight when the dust settles, the silence hits, and it's still kind of unclear what actually happened to those who were in the vicinity.

They might whisper. They might question. That's fine. They don't have to understand. They'll feel the difference soon enough when the meetings start running smoother, information starts flowing again, and momentum returns.

One day soon, they'll walk into the building and it will feel noticeably lighter.

Good people start pulling in closer and performing up to their potential again when they see that leadership has their back. They watched as you protected the baby and removed the danger. And they'll never forget it.

You can't have a healthy culture with culture bandits inside. You can't scale a business that tolerates sabotage. And you can't lead with wisdom if you're afraid to act. It's only when you've cleared the town that you can finally have peace.

Sure, there will always be another storm on the horizon, but you'll be ready for it. Meanwhile your people will be able to do their best work without fear. You'll hear laughter in the halls again, and you'll all sleep better at night, knowing the baby's safe and the business is healthy.

From Ponying Up to Powering Up

By now you've learned what it takes to build a pony-up culture where people show up, saddle up, and take ownership of their part of the ride. You've seen how alignment, accountability, and courage create motion, and how removing the culture bandits keeps that motion clean. That's the foundation, and yet it's not the finish line.

Part 4 is where the culture starts to generate power that compounds on itself. A powerful culture doesn't just hold the line. In a powerful culture, people are committed to excellence and ready to jump into action and take risks, even if it means failing from time to time. A powerful culture stays true to its principles and upholds integrity.

So if part 3 was about taking responsibility and getting all your horses pointed in the same direction, part 4 is about learning how to make them run together and not give up when the going gets tough.

PART 4

Creating a Powerful Culture

Part 4 is where we stop talking about culture like it's a poster on a wall and start treating it like it's the engine of the whole outfit—because it is. You'll learn what excellence looks like and how one shift, by starting your goal at 100%, can transform your entire team. You'll also learn how to build a culture that rewards smart risks, holds tight to principles under pressure, and calls people to bring their best every single day. And we'll finish with The Dirty Dozen, a straight-shooting letter to those just starting out in their careers.

Chapter 13

The Best Pledge™

Every great organization has a pulse that can be felt the second you walk through the door. It might be calm and confident or chaotic and confused. In the companies I've led, I've worked hard to instill a quiet, steady commitment that runs like a current through everyone from the CEO to the newest hire. And what is the commitment to?

Showing up every day as the best version of ourselves doing the best work of our lives—together. I call this commitment the Best Pledge, and it's the cornerstone of a powerful culture.

When a company truly embraces the Best Pledge, the energy changes. People walk faster and with more purpose. They stand straighter, talk differently, and make confident eye contact. The current humming through the place says, "We're all playing at the top of our game right now."

That current of energy is important because energy sells. It's contagious. People want to follow people who are excited and deeply invested in their organization. When you build a culture that honors doing your best, that energy multiplies.

So how do you make this happen? How do you create a culture where each individual is committed to being their best every day? That's what I'm going to show you in this chapter.

It Starts at the Top

In every culture, leadership sets the tone. You can't expect a team to give their best if the people at the top are too busy shooting the breeze around the hitching post to show up as their best. The Best Pledge must be modeled by the leadership team first to catch on all the way down the line.

The Best Pledge also fits right in with the structure first, people second model. When the business has the right organizational structure first and the right people are in the right seats, it's much easier for everyone to commit to doing the best work of their careers. And I do mean everyone. The Best Pledge sets a standard that ripples through the entire company. The goal is for everyone, at the same time, to be playing at the top of their game.

Someone playing at the top of their game isn't the same as someone exhausting themselves in the pursuit of perfection. The Best Pledge isn't a way to try to get your people to perform miracles or defy gravity. It's about refusing to settle for "good enough" and you quietly push each day to be a little better than yesterday.

Like I said, when your team sees you model that kind of commitment, it becomes contagious. That's when the organization's undercurrent starts to change, and excellence becomes an underlying theme.

That kind of excellence can't be manufactured. You can't just print it in a handbook or hang it on the wall. It's something that has to start inside each individual from the top of the org chart to the front line. Because before a company can do its best work, each person inside it has to decide to *be* their best self.

The Best Version of You

Every person who walks into your business brings more than their job title. They bring their habits, their beliefs, their home life, their health, and the list goes on and on. The truth is, nobody leaves their real life in their saddlebags when they come to work. So if we want excellence inside the business, we have to care about the whole person, not just the employee.

That makes the Best Pledge a professional standard *and* a personal one too. When I look across the table at the teams I work with, I ask each person to consider whether they're the best version of themselves right now at work, at home, and in their communities. I want them to reflect on that for a moment, because being your best doesn't stop when you clock out. I want your family to like that you work here. I want them to see you coming home better because you're part of something that values integrity, effort, and growth.

Now being "your best" doesn't mean being bulletproof. Life happens. People go through seasons of loss, illness, burnout, new babies, and aging parents. Sometimes the kindest thing you can do for someone is help them redefine what their "best" is for a while.

There's an old Arthur L. Williams line I love: "All you can do is all you can do. But all you can do is enough."[9]

Most people read that and think it's permission to coast, but it's not. What it really means is when someone is giving everything they honestly have in a season, it's enough. As a leader, sometimes that means lowering the load and redistributing it for a bit for someone who's struggling. Sometimes it means challenging someone who's gotten too comfortable to step it back up.

Either way, caring comes first. You can't crush people into excellence. You can only lead them there. Of course, leading people toward their best doesn't stop at caring.

Sometimes it means drawing a hard line and calling things out when they don't line up with the values you say you stand for. A true culture of excellence isn't built on comfort. It's built on character and courage.

Character and Courage

If you want a culture that lasts, integrity has to matter more than convenience.

I once had two top guys on my team who led strong departments. One was new, and one had been around a while. I suspected that when the more established team leader traveled, he did things his wife wouldn't have appreciated. I wasn't a fan of that. I'd even talked to him about it before.

---

[9] Arthur L. Williams Jr., *All You Can Do Is All You Can Do But All You Can Do Is Enough!* (New York: Nelson, 1988).

"Hey, look," I said, "that doesn't meet the Best Pledge we have here. You're affiliated with this company, and I really would prefer you not do that stuff. I don't feel comfortable with it, and I really wish you'd reconsider that kind of behavior."

He just smiled. "It doesn't affect my work," he said, clearly indicating that the subject was closed. What more could I say?

Some weeks later, I was with both team leaders on a business trip to Las Vegas. Based on what I'd already experienced with the long-standing team leader, I wondered if things were about to get dicey. Turns out, I wasn't wrong.

I hopped in the backseat of the van from the Las Vegas airport to the hotel, letting the two of them sit in the row in front of me. I was looking forward to getting checked into the hotel and having some downtime that evening when I realized the other two had much different plans—plans to go out and find some female companionship. For a moment, I sat there stunned. Then I spoke up.

"Y'all turn around and look me in the eye," I said. They both turned in their seats, and I continued. "I want to make this real clear to y'all. If you *ever* put me in a situation where you expect me to lie on your behalf to your wife or your kids, I'm gonna tell them the truth. You better not do this kind of stuff in my line of sight; I don't want anything to do with it."

They glanced guiltily at each other, then away. But I wasn't done yet.

"We came out here to work. I don't see any reason that if you would do that to your wife and kids, what in the world would you do to me or to each other or this company? At some point, you're going to get caught, and it's going to be a mess. And if I get drawn into it, I'm going to flat out tell the truth. I'm not gonna lie for y'all."

Stunned, they just looked at me for a moment. Then the newer guy said, "Well what would you have us do?"

"Don't do this crap! And especially don't do it at work in my line of sight."

That's what courage looks like in leadership. You don't have to make a public scene, but you do have to stand up for what's right in the moment with clarity and conviction. If you let small compromises slide behind closed doors, they'll eventually walk right through the swinging doors of your organization, pull up a bar stool, and make themselves at home.

A leader can't preach excellence at noon and then act like the rules don't apply after dinner. Your people are always watching, and they can spot inconsistency a mile away. But when people know they can trust you to tell the truth and do the right thing, they'll follow you through anything.

And when everyone in the organization starts holding that same line, something *powerful* happens. You no longer have to police values because people start protecting them for you. That's when you know the Best Pledge has taken root.

Holding the line on integrity has to translate into how the business actually runs. You can't have a company that talks about excellence and then builds policies that assume failure. The culture of the Best Pledge has to show up in your systems, your expectations, and the way you handle people when life happens. And here's how to make that start happening.

Building the Best Pledge into the System

Running a business that operates at its best doesn't mean chasing every exception. It means building your systems for the day-to-day and trusting your leaders to handle the one-offs. I've always said you should run your company using the 80/20 rule. Build for the 80%—the bread-and-butter operations that keep things humming—and deal with the other 20% individually.

Unfortunately, most businesses do the opposite. They write policies for every possible outlier. Someone makes a mistake or goes through a hard time, and suddenly there's a new rule carved in stone to make sure it never happens again. Before long, you've got a binder full of rules designed for 2% of situations that rarely ever happen. That kind of environment chokes out excellence.

The Best Pledge demands trust. You hire good people, you give them clear expectations, and you let them do their jobs. When something unusual comes up, like death in the family, an illness, or a mistake made in good faith, you handle it human-to-human. You don't build a new system around it. Caring doesn't always have to be codified in policy.

For example I once had a woman on my team who was returning from maternity leave after her first child. I had seen my wife go through it and knew it could be tough. Many moms face that tug-of-war between loving their work and wanting to be home with their babies. So I told my managers to check in with her after two weeks into her maternity leave to see how she was doing. If she needed to ease back into work after her leave was over, and if they could offer her 20 hours but still get paid for 40.

You'd have thought I'd suggested we move the company to Mars. Everyone looked at me like I was crazy. They couldn't believe I'd do that. But if someone on your team is struggling and you can do something to help, why wouldn't you?

You can't make a policy for every act of care. You build systems sturdy enough to handle the normal and flexible enough to handle the human. Once you've integrated the Best Pledge into your systems, the next step is making sure it starts *before* someone ever joins the team. In order to protect your powerful culture, the Best Pledge shouldn't come as a surprise to someone after they've been hired. It should be part of the conversation from the very beginning.

Hiring with the Pledge in Mind

The Best Pledge should get introduced in the interview chair.

By the time you're talking to a candidate, your organization already has its structure in place and the right seats defined. Now the question is simple: Is this person capable of being their best in that seat?

That's where you introduce the Best Pledge. You don't have to hard sell it or make it sound like a creed. You set clear expectations. I might say something like, "In this role, we're looking for someone committed to being the best version of themselves and doing the best work of their career. Is there anything going on in your life right now that would keep you from giving your best?"

It's not an interrogation. It's an act of respect. You're letting them know what kind of culture they're walking into and giving them the chance to be honest about where they are. Sometimes the timing isn't right. The Best Pledge allows them to bow out gracefully if it's not. And sometimes that question gives someone the exact motivation they need to rise to the challenge.

For existing teams, the Best Pledge can also serve as a reset button. When I come into a company that's already running, I talk to the team like we're starting fresh. I tell them, "The past is the past. From here on out, we're committing to doing the best work of our careers together."

That kind of restart wipes the slate clean and creates alignment fast. It tells people that excellence isn't a one-time campaign— it's the new operating standard.

Whether you're interviewing a new hire or reigniting an existing team, the message should be the same. "We're all going to play at the top of our game and at the same time." When you set that tone from the start, something powerful happens. The best culture stops being a leadership initiative and becomes a shared heartbeat.

Once the team understands what the best looks like collectively, the next question becomes deeply personal.

How do *I* become the kind of person who can live out the Best Pledge every day?

No matter how good your systems are, your business will only be as strong as the people steering it. And that starts with mastering yourself.

Riding the "You" Horse

One of the most fulfilling things you'll ever learn in life is how to ride the *you* horse.

Here's what I mean by that. From the moment you're born until the day you die, you're riding one horse—*you*. You can fall off, get back on, get better at riding, or make a mess of it for a while…but you don't get to trade horses. This is the one you've got for the entire journey.

I've been riding the Mel horse my whole life. Sometimes I've handled it well. Other times, I've ended up in the dirt wondering what just happened. But every time I climb back on, I know I've got a little more control, a little more awareness, and a little more humility about the road ahead.

The same is true for you. Your effectiveness as a spouse, parent, leader, follower, and teammate is directly tied to how well you ride your horse. The goal is to be present and intentional, perfection not required. The way you show up in life is entirely unique to you. No one else on the planet has your exact mix of strengths, weaknesses, quirks, and gifts. That's what makes you valuable. But it also means that learning to ride your *you* horse is part of the job description.

When you understand that, The Best Pledge takes on a new level of meaning. It's not only a commitment to do your best work. It's a commitment to be your best self. You can't lead a team effectively if you're not leading yourself well first.

The tricky part is that the same gifts that make you great often come with equal and opposite challenges. Maybe you're decisive but impatient; visionary but easily distracted; loyal but sometimes too slow to make a tough call. Every strength has a shadow. Mastering your *you* horse means learning to lead both parts of yourself—the power and the pitfalls—with honesty and grace.

That's why I always tell my teams that before we talk about riding together, they have to learn how to sit in their own saddles. And don't try to do it alone. The best way to ride the *you* horse is to stay connected to your Creator. He designed the horse. He knows the terrain. Read your Bible. Talk to God. Learn how to resemble Him in the way you live, lead, and love.

When people start mastering their own ride, the culture comes alive. You'll see it in the way they handle pressure, in the way they talk to each other, and in the calm confidence that starts to replace chaos. The Best Pledge becomes real when it's personal. Being your worst self is not an option in a culture of excellence.

So saddle up. Learn to ride your horse well. The better you get at leading yourself, the easier it is to lead others and the more powerful your entire organization becomes.

Once people start learning to ride their own horse, something else incredible happens. They stop competing with each other and start *protecting* each other. The energy shifts from *me* to *we*. And that's when the Best Pledge moves beyond personal responsibility and becomes a shared standard.

But for that to work, the environment has to be a safe place to speak up, challenge others, and grow. A culture of excellence can't thrive in silence.

How the Best Pledge Spreads Through an Organization

It is hard to get a company to embrace and execute best practice when people are being their worst selves. One person operating as their worst self can lead to a team of people working as their worst selves. It begins to feel like the slope of the trail you're on took a steep upward pitch. Those who are dedicated to self-improvement, and those who aren't, are pulling in two different directions.

When people learn how to ride their own *you* horse, something powerful begins to happen, and it doesn't stop with the individual. A culture of excellence never starts as a group project. It starts with one person making a private decision to be his or her best today. That decision creates the initial spark, but in order for the Best Pledge to filter its way through the entire organization, the spark needs to become a flame. In order for that to happen, the spark must spread from one to many, like this:

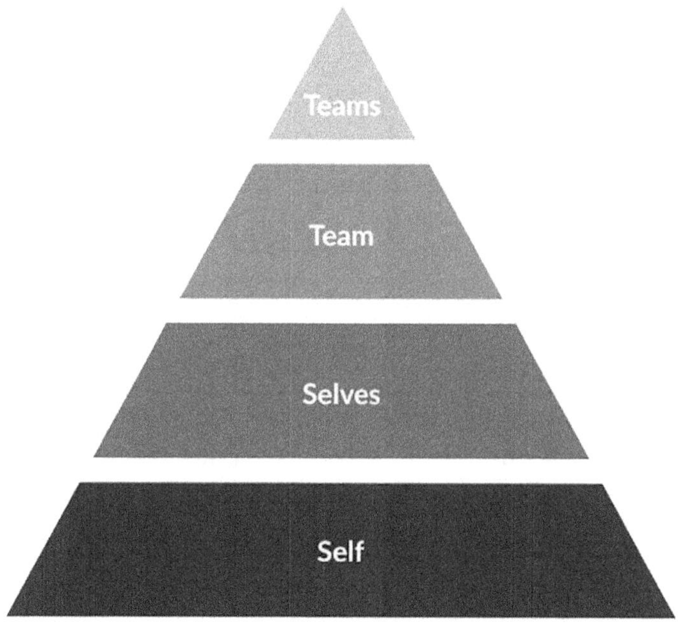

In every winning company I've ever led, the spark always begins with *self* as one person chooses to show up as the best version of themselves while rejecting self-gratification and embracing self-improvement. One person refusing to let their worst habits steer their life or their work can be powerfully impactful to the people around them.

From there, the spark is caught by others. Multiple people inside a department start working together and trying to be their best selves at the same time. This is where momentum starts. When people realize the person next to them is trying as hard as they are, trust forms fast. Energy rises, and drama fades into the background.

Then the flame catches and spreads to an entire team. Once a department is full of people committed to their individual best, the team stops behaving like a collection of separate riders and starts acting like a single unit. Communication sharpens and fewer things fall through the cracks. When everyone is already holding themselves accountable, peer accountability becomes natural instead of confrontational. The team begins to row in unison.

When enough individual teams catch fire toward the same vision, a company becomes dangerous in a good way. When several departments are all operating at their best, you get the equivalent impact of an orchestra making beautiful music together. Sales might be the brass section, operations the percussion, and finance the strings. They each have their own parts to play, but they're no longer competing for volume. They're listening to the same tempo, watching the same conductor, and playing the same piece of music. And when that happens, the sound is unmistakable. It's excellence at scale.

This is how The Best Pledge becomes more than a personal promise. It becomes a cultural current. A business can't jump straight to alignment at the company level if individuals inside it still haven't mastered themselves. The culture is only as strong as the people inside. But when Self grows into Selves, and Selves grows into Team, and Team grows into Teams, best practice stops living on a whiteboard and starts living inside the walls.

Here's the secret: This is how you get true traction. This is where leverage comes from, and your business system gets pushed all the way to the ground level. It can't be done with inspirational wall art, motivational speeches, or complicated dashboards. It can only be done by building a business full of people who refuse to be their worst selves, who take pride in being their best selves, and who bring that commitment into every room they walk into. When that happens, it's your job as the leader to make it safe for everyone to be their best.

Make It Safe to Be Your Best

When a team truly embraces the Best Pledge, the accountability stops coming only from the top. It starts happening between peers.

You'll know the culture is working when someone on your team can look at a coworker and say, "Hey, you're better when you do it this way," and it's received as encouragement, not criticism.

I had a woman who worked for me once who was incredibly talented. She was as sharp as they come, but she could rub people the wrong way. She wasn't afraid to speak her mind, especially to me. One day she pulled me aside after a meeting and said, "You know, Mel, the best *you* speaks in the affirmative, not the negative."

I stood there for a second, blinking at her. She wasn't wrong. I'd been framing things in terms of what we *didn't* want to happen instead of what we *did*. She was right. It *is* more powerful to lead with the positive. I told her thank you on the spot.

That's what a healthy culture looks like. People can challenge each other upward without fear when they know it's safe. They can call each other to a higher standard without worrying that it'll get them fired or labeled as difficult.

In a true best culture, nobody wants to let each other down. That's the power of mutual respect and shared commitment. Everyone's pulling in the same direction; when leaders make it safe to tell the truth, the truth starts to flow freely. Collaboration sharpens, performance accelerates, and people start to genuinely enjoy coming to work again.

The goal is a culture so strong, so steady, and so rooted in mutual care that doing your best stops being an instruction and starts being instinct.

The Challenge

At the end of the day, the Best Pledge is a choice. It's not a one-time meeting, company slogan, or clever initiative from leadership. It's a decision you make every single day to show up as your best self, to lead with integrity, and to lift up the people around you.

You don't need permission to do that. You don't need a title or a fancy office. You just need the willingness to own your space and ride your horse well. Being your worst self isn't an option in a culture of excellence. You suck otherwise. And who wants to suck?

Every morning when you walk through that door, you have an opportunity to make your workplace stronger, steadier, and more alive. When every person makes the same choice to be their best, do their best, and bring out the best in others, that's when the Best Pledge becomes unstoppable.

So go do it. Be the person who raises the bar just by walking in the room. Challenge yourself, encourage others, and lead with character.

Your team, your family, and your community all deserve the best you.

By the time you've got the right people in the right seats and the Best Pledge culture of accountability built, you start to feel the engine humming. But that's when the real test begins. Because growth doesn't come from coasting on smooth pavement. It comes from hitting a few bumps and keeping the throttle steady anyway. Every great culture has to learn how to ride through the wrecks. The goal isn't to avoid every fall; it's to build a team that knows how to get back up, straighten the handlebars, and keep moving. That's where we're headed next.

If You're Not Wrecking, You're Not Riding

When I was 11 and my brother was 15, we spent many weekends at our uncle's farm tearing up the woods behind his house on dirt bikes. They probably weren't street legal, and they definitely weren't safe, but we loved it. Being four years older, my brother was always four steps and about forty bruises ahead of me. Whatever he was doing, I wanted to be doing.

One day he took off down the trail like his hair was on fire and left me choking on his exhaust. I tried to keep up, but I was more cautious. I slowed down to ride over a root and ease around a tree. I watched as he disappeared over a rise at full throttle, knowing I'd never catch up.

Twenty minutes later, he was back with his knuckles split, elbow bleeding, and shirt torn—wearing the biggest grin I'd ever seen. He pulled up beside me, killed the engine, and said, "Man, that was awesome!"

"Did you wreck *again*?" I asked, staring at his handlebars that were bent enough to make me nervous. I, on the other hand, looked like I'd just left Sunday school. There wasn't a speck of mud or scratch on me.

He nodded proudly. "Yeah, I laid it down right past the creek."

I shook my head, part concerned and part impressed. "You're bleeding."

He looked down at his arm, wiped the blood on his jeans with a grin, and said, "If you're not wrecking, you're not riding."

Then he kicked that old bike back to life and took off again.

That line—if you're not wrecking, you're not riding—has always stuck with me.

At the time, I thought he was crazy. Who wants to wreck on purpose? Years later after enough business meetings, bad hires, lost deals, and busted plans, I realized the phrase doesn't only apply to riding dirt bikes. It applies to life and business, too.

Of course this wrecking and riding advice assumes that all previous chapters of the book have been implemented. What is great about uncommon sense is that it does build. Some things need to be done before the others are implemented. In a structurally broken, cats-barking, worst-self, bandit-ridden town, wrecking and riding is a horrible idea.

My brother taught me an important lesson about taking risks and putting in full effort. He reminded me that in order to really make progress, you have to get in the game hard enough that you might actually fall down. Most people spend their careers polishing the bike instead of riding it. They want clean numbers, safe choices, and predictable outcomes. But here's the truth my brother understood before I did: Playing it safe is the slowest way to fail.

And he was right. If you're not wrecking once in a while, you're probably not really riding. Here are the nine lessons I learned from my brother about wrecking and riding.

Lesson 1: Playing It Safe Is the Real Risk

It took me a long time to realize that *safety* can be its own kind of collision course. When you ride timidly, you may think you're avoiding pain, but all you're really doing is avoiding progress.

The wild west of business doesn't reward clean bikes. While the cautious are circling the parking lot, someone else is already halfway up the mountain. I used to think the safest employees were the best ones. Then I realized they were usually the most afraid. They're afraid of being wrong, getting in trouble, or making a mess. But fear doesn't build companies. It stalls them. The biggest risk you can take is pretending that standing still is safe.

Lesson 2: Be Calculating, Not Careless

There's a difference between wrecking and reckless. What my brother taught me back when we were kids wasn't about being wild. It was about being *willing*. The line between control and chaos is the heart of innovation. If you want true innovation and progress in your business, you must create a space where your people can take smart risks.

Provide the tools and the training.

Make sure they're prepared for the trail ahead and that they understand what winning looks like.

Then let them ride.

Lesson 3: Fast Fail, Fast Fix

If you're going to fall, why not get out there and fall quickly so you can get back up quicker? And don't leave the bike in the ditch and call it a loss. Straighten the handlebars, knock the mud off the wheels, and keep moving.

A fast-fail culture is a *learning* culture. You try. You miss. Then you fix it and move on. Blaming and complaining doesn't fix anything. The real fix comes from curiosity as people dive into what happened. Anytime you try something new, it's like riding a new trail. The first few runs are messy, but as you ride, you learn where every root and rut is. Next time, you'll glide right through.

Fast fail, fast fix isn't about rushing. It's about setting a standard and creating a rhythm. When you commit to moving fast, you'll learn fast and make positive adjustments quickly. If you want speed in business, you can't wait for every turn to feel safe. You have to be smart about it, of course, but trust that you're supported by your team, and then take the turn anyway.

Lesson 4: Delegate and Trust

If you want to keep growing as a leader, at some point you're going to need to hand somebody else the bike. That's delegation, and that's where a lot of leaders flinch. The delegation and trust equation looks like this:

Freedom + responsibility = trust

Looks simple, right? So why is it so hard? We say we want people to take ownership, but it's not always easy to allow it. Deep down we don't want anyone to throw a wrench in the well-oiled machine we've built. We hand over the keys only to stand six inches away giving play-by-play instructions. That's not delegation. That's babysitting.

If you've hired well, trained well, and set clear expectations, you've earned the right to trust that you've prepared your people well. Don't delegate and levitate, like I talked about in chapter 4. Give your people permission to act without you hanging over their shoulder. Make it *safe* to ride hard. You'll never know what your people are capable of until you stop holding the handlebars for them.

Lesson 5: Course Correct Daily

Even the best riders drift off the trail. That's part of the ride. Business itself doesn't always operate in a straight line. It's more like a zigzag or rollercoaster. Stay calm, course correct daily, and keep moving.

Don't wait until you're in the ditch to check the map. Practice the connect-the-dots decision-making you learned in chapter 9. When you make daily course correction part of your culture, people stop hiding mistakes. They bring them up early because they know you're not there to scold. You're there to help them stay upright.

Daily course correction also helps your people learn how to read the trail before the next curve. Things might get a little offkilter, but it's easily correctable when you assess progress daily. Then you can nudge things in the right direction, course correcting without bringing progress to a complete halt.

Lesson 6: Give Away the Handlebars

One of the smartest things I ever learned as a leader was to give away as much of my job as I could. Most people hear that and think that sounds lazy, but it's not. It's good leadership.

The more you hang onto, the slower your company moves. When everything has to pass through your hands, *you* become the bottleneck. But when you start pushing responsibility down and handing off pieces of the ride, something powerful happens.

People rise. They get better. They start to see what you see.

I've always said the person at the top should be working themselves out of a job. If you've built your team right, there'll come a day when they don't need you to ride every mile with them. The primary goal for my teams is for them to get so good at this that they don't need me anymore.

If the place falls apart when I leave, then I wasn't leading well. A strong leader gives people freedom *and* credit. When a team member does great work, a leader shines the light on them. When they miss, a leader stands beside them. You can't lose when you lead like that, because people don't forget who believed in them enough to hand them the handlebars.

Lesson 7: Choose Excellence Over Perfection

There's a difference between excellence and perfection. Perfection sounds noble, but it's a trap. It freezes people and kills speed. When you send your team out to chase perfection, they'll start second-guessing every move, rewriting every report, and polishing every detail until the window of opportunity slams shut.

Excellence is different. Excellence says, "We're going to do the best job possible with what we've got, and we're going to deliver on time." Excellence matters more because it's measurable, repeatable, and contagious.

A team that chases perfection ends up cautious.

A team that chases excellence ends up confident, and confidence is what turns wrecks into lessons. You learn, you fix, and you keep moving. You do it better the next time. And all along, you're creating the kind of gradual mastery that only comes from doing.

Lesson 8: Give the Credit Away

If you need all the credit, you're not ready to lead. Leadership isn't about standing on the podium. It's about helping everybody else cross the finish line. The good shepherd doesn't need the glory. He gives it to the flock. If your team trusts that you'll give them the win, they'll ride harder than you ever could by yourself.

Give honor where honor is due, and a powerful culture will cement itself into your business. Don't take someone's win away from them. I've watched too many leaders flatten their own teams by stealing credit for the sake of optics or ego. What they don't realize is that they're sawing off the very branch they're sitting on. You want your people to fight for the company? Fight for them first, and give them room to shine. Let them own their success. When a big win comes through, turn the spotlight outward.

The funny thing is, when you give credit away, it always comes back multiplied. You'll have a team full of riders who aren't just loyal to the paycheck. They're loyal to *you*. They'll bleed for the mission, not because they have to, but because they *want* to.

Lesson 9: Predictable Wrecks and Better Riders

If you've been leading long enough, you already know that there will never come a day when your business will be wreck-free. Early on the wrecks are loud and messy. Later, the wrecks get quieter. By then, the riders have changed too. They've learned to lean into the turns instead of overcorrecting. They've learned how to slide, recover, and keep their balance under pressure.

That's what I mean by *predictable wrecks*. They still happen, but they don't scare anybody anymore. You can see them coming, manage the impact, and move forward without losing momentum. When your people start wrecking differently, you know they're growing. They're not making the same mistakes. They're making *better* ones that stretch them and teach them something new.

A mature organization isn't one without failure. It's one that learns as it falls and recovers quickly. That's the kind of company you want—one that doesn't crumble at the first wobble. You can't buy that kind of culture. You have to build it one scar, one scrape, and one lesson at a time.

The Joy of the Ride

I still think about that day in the woods sometimes. There I am, sitting on a perfectly clean bike while my brother stood there covered in mud and grinning like he'd just conquered the world.

At the time, I thought he was crazy. But looking back, he was right all along.

He wasn't celebrating the fall.

He was celebrating the ride.

Life and leadership is a journey to stay moving. You're going to tip over. You're going to scrape your knees, bend a few handlebars, and question why you got on the bike in the first place. But when you look back, you'll realize those were the moments that shaped you, rather than the easy stretches or smooth roads.

When I think about the best seasons of my career, they all have one thing in common: We were riding hard. We were trying new things, pushing limits, and learning fast. When the dust settled, the team was tighter, and the company was stronger.

The ride is worth it. If you're sitting clean and unscathed today, maybe it's time to twist the throttle again. Try something bold. Delegate something scary. Trust somebody new. Lead by example how it should be done. You might lay it down once or twice, but you'll be alive in the process.

Business isn't meant to be parked. It's meant to stay in motion.

And when it's all said and done, I hope you can look back, like my brother did that day, and say, "Yeah, I wrecked a few times. But man…wasn't that a great ride?"

Chapter 15

The Last Good Guy in the Room Never Puts Down His Gun

There's a phrase I've said for years that you're going to want to remember. If you're the last good guy in the room, never put down your gun.

You and I both know I'm not talking about a literal gun. And of course I'm using the word "guy" in the colloquial sense, meaning man or woman. There's something inside you that makes you stand your ground when something's not right. Call it your principles, ethics, or moral pine. Leaders need to have a willingness to step forward when everybody else in the room suddenly finds the ceiling tiles really interesting.

Whether you want the role or not, there will be a moment for you as the leader when you realize you're the only one with any integrity left in the room. Surprise! Like it or not, you just became the shepherd, the person in charge of leading and protecting your organization. The moment there's a rattlesnake holding everyone hostage in the conference room and no one else is moving, the responsibility lands on your shoulders. And your job becomes very, very simple.

Stand firm. One of my best tools for standing your ground is called The Razor™.

The Razor: How Good Guys Win Hard Conversations

Let me tell you about one of the most unexpected lessons I ever learned about standing your ground. Back in 1997, the leadership of USA Mobile, the company I'd been transforming from the ground up for the past five years, had retired or moved on to other endeavors. That leadership team loved me. I was their golden child, but things were about to change for young Mel.

A new boss was brought in. Now I get it. This guy didn't know me from anybody, and, as I like to say, I wasn't his dog. This guy was brilliant and tough, and he happened to be a former captain of the Harvard debate team. I realized early on that I was in a whole new ball game. In one of my early interactions with him, he ate my lunch when I called him to negotiate a raise. It was a total disaster. He dismantled my entire argument like he was shelling peanuts.

I'm stubborn as a mule though, so I asked for a face-to-face meeting, booked a flight to North Carolina where his offices were, and prepared to walk into battle. The truth is, I was walking straight into a gunfight armed with a butter knife. But I wasn't about to give up.

Then something happened that I still can't fully explain.

The night before the meeting, I stopped at Landry's Seafood for dinner. As I parked, a gentleman with red hair stepped out of a white pickup at the same time I did. We reached the door together, and the hostess asked, "Table for two?" I looked at the guy, shrugged, and said, "Sure." That wasn't like me. I've always been a lone wolf when I travel, so this was way out of character.

We sat down and made small talk, but within minutes, he looked straight through me and said, "Something's on your mind."

I figured there was no harm in talking to a stranger I'd never see again, so I told him I was about to face off with a brilliant boss, and I needed to make my case for better compensation. As I talked, he listened intently, then said something that changed my life.

"Have you ever heard of 'The Razor?'"

I shook my head. I had not.

"Okay," he said. "I'll show you how it works, but you have to promise to only use it for good."

That sounded serious, and I agreed. I had no plans to go culture bandit on my new boss anyway. He pulled a napkin toward him and started sketching. What he showed me changed the way I negotiate to this day.

The Razor is a simple negotiation tactic made up of three strong, simple points that you repeat in a disciplined, circular rhythm no matter what the other person says.

That's it. Just three. It was so simple, but I could tell right away that it would be highly effective.

The red-haired gentleman helped me come up with and sharpen my three points. We practiced until I felt confident about it, then I turned away to ask for the check. When I turned back seconds later, he was gone. I looked down the bar, which was the only way in and out of Landry's, and there was no sign of him. I even ran out to the parking lot; there was no trace of the red-headed angel or his white truck.

There was no way he'd have been able to leave that fast without me seeing him. I didn't know what to make of it.

The next morning, I walked into my boss's office with The Razor in hand. I stayed calm and focused on my three points. No matter what my new boss said, I didn't budge. At one point he actually called for a break. That's when I knew The Razor was working.

In the end, we came to a stalemate.

"I underestimated you," he said. And I got the raise.

When you're the last good guy in the room, you don't survive the moment by being louder or flashier. You survive it by being prepared, disciplined, steady, and focused.

Don't pass the problem up the chain. Don't pretend not to see it or wait for someone else to fix it. And *definitely* don't worship the problem by letting it get bigger while you look for new ways to avoid it. Draw your gun and hit the problem square between the eyes.

Are you interested in learning The Razor yourself? If you promise to only use it for good, I'll teach it to you. I've recorded a 19-minute video that walks you through how to use The

Razor step-by-step. You can watch it on my book website. Flip to the Resources section of this book for the link to the website.

And since we're talking about being the shepherd, we need to slow down here and look at what that actually means. This isn't some heroic movie moment where the music swells and everything feels noble. Most of the time, being the shepherd shows up in ordinary, uncomfortable situations where you'd give anything for someone else to handle it. But they won't, and that's exactly why you have to.

You *not* being the shepherd should not be an option, yet some people in leadership have no problem abdicating that role. Let's talk about what it looks like to put down your gun.

What It Looks Like to Put Down Your Gun

The world today is scared of conflict. Nobody wants to hurt somebody else's feelings or end up on the wrong side of a lawsuit. Heaven forbid you get stuck on the crossfire of one of those societal hot-button topics. People look around, see a tough situation, and their first instinct is to go hide under their desk and hope the problem burns itself out without singeing their eyebrows. But by not acting, leaders get soft at exactly the moment they need to be steel.

Most leaders don't fail because they're evil. They fail because they put their gun down the minute things get uncomfortable. They duck. They delay. They hand the problem up the ladder like it's a hot potato they only agreed to hold for two seconds. And then they wonder why their team doesn't trust them, why morale's slipping, and why the culture feels like it's being held together with bailing wire.

You might think, "Oh, I'd never do that! I'd never put down my gun." I certainly hope not. But putting down your gun happens long before the big dramatic moment. It happens in the small stuff, like

- threatening a consequence you never intend to enforce,
- pretending interdepartmental issues don't exist, or
- hiding in your office instead of dealing with someone who's undermining your culture.

Those are all examples of putting the gun down. And the minute you do it, your credibility evaporates.

Remember the executive in Pensacola who called me in to fire his employee from chapter 3? Instead of handling it like a leader himself, he brought me in. That was a big mistake. If you are the leader on site, and you've got the authority and responsibility to deal with a personnel issue, you don't call Daddy to come do it.

Did I do it? Yes. I was in the region, so I went. I got down there, ready to do the job he should have done, and he has the nerve to try to talk me out of firing the guy. What sense does that make? He put the gun down, handed it to me, and then when I picked it up, he reached over and tried to push my arm away.

If you're supposed to be the one to fire someone, then you fire them. If you're supposed to confront the behavior, then you confront it. If you're supposed to lead the meeting, then you lead the meeting. Putting your gun down is the fastest way to turn yourself into someone people politely tolerate but never follow.

No one follows a leader who bluffs. No one respects a leader who floats threats. And no one trusts a leader who disappears when it's time to act.

Want to know what kills cultures faster than anything else? Faster than a culture bandit? It's a leader who refuses to do the hard thing at the moment the hard thing needs to be done. That right there is a culture killer.

Once your people learn that you're all bark and no bite, it doesn't matter how nice you are, how smart you are, or how many years you've been there. Your influence is gone. You can lose it in one moment of cowardice, and spend the next ten years trying to claw it back. If you're going to be the last good guy in the room, you can't put the gun down. Not for any reason. Not even once.

That's not leadership. That's surrender.

Is it heavy? Yes. But it's what you need to do if you really want to step into your role as a shepherd of your people. This shouldn't be taken lightly. Being the shepherd is a whole different level of responsibility. And it doesn't start with power, but with protection.

Let's talk about what being a shepherd actually looks like.

The Shepherd Principle

Now here's where people get this whole "gun" thing wrong. They hear me talk about standing your ground and doing the hard thing, and they think I'm talking about charging into the room with guns blazing like some kind of overzealous cowboy. No. That's not the spirit of this at all.

Being the last good guy in the room is not about aggression. It's about protection. That's why I use the word shepherd.

Think about a shepherd in the real world. He's not out there peacocking around, yelling at the sheep. He spends 99% of the time watching with full attention to make sure the flock is safe and moving the right direction.

But when the rattlesnake shows up, the shepherd stands up. Every business will have to face down a rattlesnake now and then. That's when the gun comes out of the holster and stays firmly in the shepherd's hand.

The thing about taking on the shepherd role is that it often happens without fanfare. Like I said at the beginning of this chapter, whether you like it or not, if you're the one standing there when something goes sideways, you're the shepherd.

There's no election or special badge. There's just you, recognizing a threat and stepping up to deal with it, no matter what it is. It might be a toxic employee spreading poison in the break room or a high-dollar client crossing lines they shouldn't cross. Maybe somebody is harassing a team member or lying and stirring up division. Sometimes the threat isn't a person at all. Sometimes it's a broken system, a bad process, or a leadership gap somewhere else in the org chart that's putting unnecessary pressure on your people.

As the shepherd, it's your job to see it first. After all, you understand what's at stake. You'll step in because you care about your flock and not because you enjoy the fight.

When you're the shepherd, you don't get the luxury of pretending something isn't happening. You don't get to wait for the perfect moment. You don't get to say, "Well, maybe this will fix itself." Shepherds who wait for problems to fix themselves wake up to dead sheep. A leader who won't protect the culture is worse than no leader at all.

People need to know deep in their bones that if something or someone dangerous shows up, you'll step forward. You'll take the hit and absorb the blow. You'll swing the stick if you have to because the safety, dignity, and livelihood of your team actually mean something to you.

Shepherds Don't Weaponize. They Steward.

Another important thing to note is that good shepherds don't use their authority to bully people or pit departments against each other. They use it to settle things down and get people talking. A good shepherd will help departments see past the surface-level drama and down into what's actually going on.

The senior chairs in a business carry real power. No matter what letters follow your name—COO, CEO, CFO, or VP— your role requires you to steward your teams well. So do you use your gun to create chaos or unity?

Most conflict isn't actually two villains fighting. Most of it is two stressed, tired, overwhelmed people running on fumes who get backed into corners by processes or pressures they didn't create. That's why a good shepherd doesn't punish first. He listens, looks deeper, and tries to understand the terrain his people are fighting on.

When the root cause is clear, he fixes the dysfunction without yelling or blaming. He protects the team while restoring order. That's the shepherd principle in action.

It's not glamorous or dramatic. You probably won't get a standing ovation for it. But if you shepherd well and consistently, your people will follow you anywhere. They know that if you're in the room, they're safe.

Not everyone in your organization *is* safe though. Now that we've talked about the shepherd, let me reintroduce you to the opposite kind of character—the culture bandit. We've talked about this character already, so we're not going to go too deep describing culture bandits in this chapter. But let me tell you a little bit about how culture bandits operate so you can see the contrast.

Culture Bandits and the Cost of Doing Nothing

If you've led anything for more than ten minutes, you've met a culture bandit. They're not always the worst performers. They can be smart and talented. Sometimes they're the person everyone thinks is harmless because they've been around a long time.

But the second you walk out of the room, culture bandits start pulling in the opposite direction. You can have an amazing leadership team pushing a vision uphill while sweating, bleeding, and selling people on the mission. Meanwhile, one culture bandit is in the break room saying, "Well I don't know why we're doing it this way," or "The execs don't even know what they're talking about" or "I heard they're planning XYZ."

That culture bandit is costing you more than any bad quarter, any lost deal, or any budget hit you're worried about. Culture bandits destroy alignment and excitement around your vision. Along comes one culture bandit and with one little whisper, can undo weeks—sometimes months—of progress.

That's why I say doing nothing is not neutral; it's destructive. If you leave the wrong person in place, I promise that you won't get the culture you deserve, and your people will suffer.

You're not just risking the business failing. You're risking the business *almost* succeeding—never quite making it, never quite breaking through—because one or two people have enough influence to keep everyone doubting at the wrong time. A culture bandit doesn't have to be malicious. They just have to be loud at the wrong moment.

The shepherd sees this. He or she knows what the cost of taking action will be, but he or she acts anyway. The shepherd knows that if you don't deal with the rattlesnake, the rattlesnake will deal with you.

And that leads me straight into one of the hardest leadership decisions I ever had to make. This one taught me how expensive it can be when you're the last good guy in the room while everyone else is asleep at the wheel.

Protecting the Business and Taking the Hit

Let me tell you a story I don't think I've ever written down before.

I was being recruited by an ERP software company to build a brand-new major accounts division. This was something they'd never done before. Up until then, they were selling to midsized and smaller operations. They were very successful, but they wanted to go after the big fish. They wanted true enterprise clients.

If that sounds exciting, it was…except for the problem big enough to sink the whole thing before it started. To build a major accounts division, you need the best of everything. You need top sales engineers, the best project managers, the most experienced coders, and the sharpest customization people.

In order to win, I had to build an expert team. Expanding the core is tricky. Where will the resources come from? Will I rob Peter to pay Paul? Is this going to fracture a good company? How can I thread the needle and create the win-win result at the speed of business before the window of opportunity closes?

The fact was, the resources would have to come from the existing core team's sales team budget. We'd be cannibalizing a department that was already performing great in their market. I was sure the existing team was not okay with that. Leadership, however, knew they had to expand the core and wanted to take the risk. They needed the enterprise division and felt like I was the guy that would figure it out. They believed I could pull it off.

This is where the shepherd principle comes in, because I could already see the rattlesnake. If I walked in and took everything I needed, I'd be hated instantly. Was I the bad guy? Not technically, and yet I would be draining the heart of the existing business to pump blood into a brand-new experiment that had zero guarantee of success. I couldn't go into it like that.

Before I ever said yes to the job, I sat down with the owner and the senior executives and told them flat-out, "This will not work unless we deal with the resource issue. I'm not taking this job on a suicide mission."

They were stunned. Nobody had said it that directly before, but I wasn't trying to be dramatic. I was trying to protect them from themselves, and I was willing to put my entire opportunity on the line before I ever accepted it. I knew that if I didn't use my leverage *before* I came on board, I wouldn't have any left once I did. Once I took the position, I'd be just another employee with a job to protect.

So I said no. And because I said no, they had to pay attention. They pulled together their senior people, and we all sat down and sorted things out. Before I ever walked through the door as a part of that company, we sat down and created a resource-sharing plan and made sure expectations were aligned all around. We agreed on what could be shared, what couldn't, and what would have to wait.

And do you know what? The plan worked. Within six months, we landed one of the top enterprise clients in their entire industry. It was a multimillion-dollar deal most people said couldn't be done.

But guess what else? Everything I predicted about resource tension came true. As the major accounts division grew, those shared resources started stretching thin. It was simple math. The same people who were supporting the mid-market clients were now being asked to support a monster enterprise project with a five-year provisioning timeline.

I could feel the strain and see the cracks forming. There was going to be a long-term cost to this, so I had another decision to make. I had every reason to stay after the big win and all the excitement. Heck, everyone wanted to work in my division because it was sexy and fun and innovative.

But staying would've taken an even bigger bite out of a core business that had been thriving long before I walked in the door. The sales team, some of them 25+ year managers of the department, were worried. They had come to trust me. And believe me, I had to really work for it. And now they could see the writing on the wall. Staying and pursuing more enterprise level accounts would crush their department, and the company would be the casualty.

Instead of going to the CEO or their bosses, they came to me. They trusted me. So I did the only right thing there was to do. I left. Although the CEO was shocked—he had no idea about the sales team's concerns—I left on great terms because the business needed the oxygen.

Years later, the major accounts division is their biggest revenue generator. They're thriving and dominating their space, but not at the expense of the mid-level accounts.

I refused to put down my gun in negotiations in that situation, but not because I personally wanted to win. I did it for the sake of doing right by the entire company. I wish I could tell you every story I have ends that nicely, but that would be a lie. Doing the right thing is necessary, and it's not always fun.

Using Power to Restore Peace, Not Create Chaos

One thing leaders often don't fully appreciate until they've made a few messes is that power itself is neutral. It isn't good or bad on its own. It simply amplifies whoever holds it. And in every organization, the senior chairs like the COO, CFO, VP, and director carry a built-in level of authority whether they want it or not. The question is never *whether* they have power. The real question is what they're using it *for*.

Some leaders use their power to stir things up, to pit departments against one another or to create little internal kingdoms where they can feel important. Those people look impressive for a while, but the trail of drama and distrust they leave behind is always the same. Under those leaders, people spend more time bracing for impact than doing their jobs. That kind of leadership is nothing more than insecurity with a gold nameplate.

A real leader uses their power to restore peace, not create chaos. And let me tell you, most of the conflict in a business isn't good versus evil. It's two overwhelmed, exhausted people clashing because something upstream is broken. Maybe their processes are terrible or they're carrying the weight of decisions someone else made. Perhaps a lack of leadership has left them fighting each other instead of the real problem. When you're the one with authority, you don't walk into that situation spoiling for a fight or pick a side before you understand what's actually going on.

I used to handle these kinds of moments all the time. Two departments would be circling each other, tensions high, everyone frustrated and confused. I'd sit them down and say, "All right, what's really happening here?" A surprising number of times, the issue wasn't about the people at the table at all. It was a rattlesnake they *didn't* see, like burnout, a broken system, an unrealistic workload, or someone else's poor leadership causing the collision. That's why shepherds don't fight the sheep. They go after the snake.

As a leader you can't sweep ownership under the rug. Sometimes the conclusion is "Neither of you is the problem. This is a system issue." Other times, it's "Buddy, you actually *are* the problem, and it stops today." Either way, the goal is always to bring people back to unity, restore order, and protect the culture. This is what will help the team get back to the mission instead of wasting emotional energy on conflict that should've been resolved weeks ago.

When you consistently use your power to create unity, fairness, and clarity instead of chaos, people notice. They start to exhale around you. They stop guarding themselves. They trust that if something goes sideways, you'll step in to help. They'll know your intention is not to intimidate or humiliate, but to make things better. They may not always love your decisions, and yet they'll respect the steadiness behind them. And once people know that your presence means the problem is finally going to get dealt with, not ignored or inflamed, your leadership becomes an anchor in the organization instead of something people have to tiptoe around.

Be the leader whose power brings people together instead of tearing them apart. When your team believes that your authority exists to protect them and not to elevate you, they'll follow you anywhere, and your culture becomes almost impossible to break.

Handling the Little Things

When people think about leadership, they usually imagine the big moments like the dramatic standoffs, the tough calls, and the pivotal decisions that make for great stories later. But the truth is, most leadership isn't dramatic at all. It's the small, unglamorous moments where nobody's watching, nobody's cheering, and nobody's handing out medals. And yet, it's in those everyday moments when your credibility is built or lost.

For years I've said that if you want to know whether someone really has leadership in them, don't watch them during the crisis. Watch them on a random Tuesday. Watch how they handle the little frictions between people, the minor misunderstandings, the process hiccups, and the tension that creeps into a team when someone's tired, stressed, or overworked. What you do with the little things determines whether your people trust you when the big things hit.

You'd be surprised how much dysfunction comes from small, ignored issues that never get addressed. A quick conversation could've solved it, and instead it festers. A misunderstanding gets blown out of proportion when nobody bothered to clarify it. Two people start snapping at each other, not because they dislike one another, but because one hasn't taken a vacation in six months and the other is drowning in responsibilities nobody seems to notice. These are the moments where a leader earns their stripes by showing attention rather than force.

I can't tell you how many times I walked into a room where two people were butting heads, only to realize neither of them was the true issue. Maybe the workload was unrealistic. Maybe someone else upstream was dropping the ball. Maybe personal stress outside of work was bleeding into how they were communicating. It didn't matter. What mattered was they needed someone to slow things down long enough to get beneath the surface instead of judging the surface.

That's why the shepherd analogy matters so much. A shepherd doesn't only protect the flock from rattlesnakes and wolves; he also pays attention to the sheep themselves. Who's limping? Who's drifting off? Who's anxious? Who's carrying more weight than they should? In business, those signs show up in little ways, like a sharp tone in a meeting, a drop in performance from someone who's normally rock-solid, a sudden defensiveness, or two people who used to get along suddenly struggling to communicate.

Those moments aren't interruptions to the real work. They are the real work.

Your willingness to handle the little things sets the tone for your entire organization. When people see you step in early, calmly, and consistently, they stop letting problems grow roots. They start bringing things to you before they explode. They feel safe enough to tell you what's actually going on instead of what they think you want to hear.

When leaders ignore the small stuff, everyone else learns to ignore it too until it becomes big stuff that costs you people, momentum, and opportunity.

Handling the little things doesn't mean micromanaging or hovering. It simply means paying attention, asking questions, and caring enough to intervene before something tiny grows teeth. It's being the kind of leader who notices the signs of strain and steps in with clarity instead of waiting until the situation requires force.

When your people understand that you care about the day-to-day dynamics as much as the big-picture goals, you create a culture where instead of getting buried, problems get resolved. That's where trust grows, unity strengthens, and your team becomes capable of doing the kind of work that changes the entire trajectory of the business.

Need a short list of how to be a good shepherd when you're the last (or first) good guy in the room? Check out the tips in the box below.

Practical Actions for Being the Last Good Guy in the Room

When you're the last good guy in the room, remember:

- Say what you mean, and mean what you say. Don't bluff.
- Follow through on consequences. If you warn it, you enforce it.
- Step in early. Small problems rarely stay small.
- Don't hand your gun upward. Handle what's yours to handle.
- Protect your people. That's your first job, not your last.
- Be willing to walk away. Leverage only works before you say yes.

> - Address rattlesnakes and culture bandits quickly. Doubt spreads faster than truth.
> - Use power to calm things down, not stir things up.
> - Look beneath the surface. Conflict is often a symptom, not the root.
> - Choose the whole business over your own success. Integrity has a long tail.
> - Don't worship the problem. Face it, deal with it, and move the team forward.
> - Stay steady. When you're consistent, people stop bracing and start trusting.

Being the last good guy in the room isn't about heroics, swagger, or ego. It's about steadiness, integrity, and caring enough to take the hit when the moment calls for it. Most of the time, it won't feel glamorous at all. In fact, the moments where you "hold your gun" are usually the moments where you'll be tempted to wish someone else—anyone else—would step in instead.

That's the nature of leadership. You don't always get to pick your moments. Sometimes the responsibility falls on you, and the only question left is whether you're going to stand your ground or shrink back.

I've learned that the people who thrive in leadership aren't the ones who love authority. They're the ones who love the people. Good leaders can see the cost of avoiding the hard thing. They know that cultures don't crumble all at once, but erode through small compromises that pile up over time.

And they refuse to be part of that erosion.

When you hold your gun and protect the culture, confront the rattlesnake, settle the unnecessary fights, and steady the team when things feel shaky, you become the kind of leader people remember. They'll trust and follow you even when you're not in the room. That is the quiet power of refusing to put your gun down.

When the day comes that you look around and realize you *are* the last good guy in the room, don't panic or duck. Don't hand it up the chain. Pull out your gun, take a breath, and do what's right.

That's what real leaders do.

Chapter 16

A Letter for Those Starting Out in Business

So you're at the beginning of your career. That means you probably haven't screwed anything up yet, not in any way that matters at least. The road ahead of you is wide open, and that's a good place to be. Reading this book now will set you on the right path early on, before you develop set patterns that won't serve you or your organization.

So before the noise of business, ego, politics, and pressure starts getting into your bloodstream, I want to hand you something simple and honest. In this chapter, I'm giving you The Dirty Dozen. These 12 lessons are things I wish someone had spelled out for me when I first stepped into the business world as a greenhorn with no idea which end of the horse was up.

Think of this as a letter from someone who's been in the trenches a long time and has the scars to prove it. What I'm about to give you aren't theories. They're hard-earned truths. If you'll take them seriously, they'll give you a real shot at a career you can be proud of.

So I present to you The Dirty Dozen.

1. Embrace Hard Work

When you're new, you're not an expert yet. I'm not trying to insult you. That's how life works. Before you gain expertise and finesse, and before you develop the instincts that only come from repetition, all you really have is raw work ethic. The good news is, at this point, hard work is enough to get you moving in the right direction.

It's like Art Williams said: "All you can do is all you can do, and all you can do is enough."[10]

That said, "all you can do" in business is a lot more than what was expected in college. So show up early, stay engaged, and do the work to gain expertise. Hard work creates competence, and competence creates confidence. There's no shortcut for that.

2. Be Coachable and Follow the System

One of the greatest advantages you have when you're new is that you don't know enough to think you know better. That's a gift, so use it. Find the people who actually know what they're doing, then follow the system *exactly* the way they teach it.

When I started at USA Mobile, I didn't know a thing about selling pagers. What I *did* know was that the people training me had kung fu. I could tell they were the real deal. So when they told me what to do, I did it without hesitation. My branch became the most successful startup in the company's history

---

[10] Williams Jr., *All You Can Do Is All You Can Do But All You Can Do Is Enough!*.

because I was coachable and did exactly what the people ahead of me taught me to do.

3. Stay Out of the Politics

You want to move up fast? Stay out of the us vs. them gossip and petty drama. Politics is where mediocre careers go to die. Keep your nose clean and your head down. Let your work speak louder than your words.

4. Don't Be Afraid to Ask for Help

There is no shame in not knowing something. What *is* embarrassing is making preventable mistakes because you were pretending you know what you're doing. Adopt the fast fail, fast fix mentality from chapter 14. If you mess up, own it. If you're confused, ask for clarification. That's how you grow faster than the people around you.

5. Don't Surprise Your Boss

Your boss should never find out about something important from someone else. Communicate all news—the good, the bad, and the ugly—early on. Leaders need time to think, plan, and help you succeed. Don't try to wow them by holding back a win for a big reveal, and don't hide a problem because you're afraid. Be transparent right away.

6. Be Excited About the Journey

Business is mostly the art of taking someone's vision and turning it into reality. The vision is the destination. The subvision is the journey. And the journey requires commitment, discipline, and a willingness to execute the best practices that make the whole thing work. Don't underestimate how powerful it is to simply do the right thing, the right way, every day. Enthusiasm for best practice is rocket fuel early in your career. After all, as Art Williams said, "People won't follow a disillusioned doggone crybaby."[11]

7. Commit to Becoming the Best Version of Yourself

You can lie to the world, but don't lie to yourself. You know when you're phoning it in. You know when you're repeating mistakes instead of learning from them. Being the best version of yourself is a daily decision you can make, so *make* it.

My granddaddy Blackwell was a man of few words. When he got older and sicker, he'd still look at us and say the same thing every time we left:

"Go do something for the cause of good every day."

8. Be "I'm Glad I Did," Not "I Wish I Would Have"

Everybody has days of reckoning and moments where your choices show up and look you in the eye. When that day comes, you want to be the person who says, "I'm glad I did," not the one sitting there whispering, "I wish I would have." Everything in this book is built to stack your odds toward the first one so you don't have to live in regret.

---

[11] *"Just Do It,"* YouTube video, 18:29, posted by *Darrin Prude,* July 3, 2014, https://youtu.be/-BXiEkddWR8?si=tPoK0tJH1s8RkFjU

9. Don't Mess with People's Money

Compensation is sacred territory, so don't play games with or manipulate it. Money might be neutral, but how you handle it tells the world everything about who you are. Don't jerk people around or keep them guessing. Be compassionate, honest, and fair. People should never feel unsafe around you financially.

10. Start Doing Your Job at Goal

Mediocrity is not a plan, and good enough shouldn't be standard. Your job begins at hitting the goal so you can go further, faster. Build the muscle of chasing the number until the number gets scared of you.

11. When Left in Charge, Take Charge

It can be scary when you are not sure exactly what to do. Instead of being tentative, be intentional. Take care of things. Solve more problems for your boss. If you want upward mobility, become the person who solves problems instead of worshiping them. Don't bring your boss a tangle of issues and a shrug. Bring the problem, the possible solutions, and your recommended path. Leaders love people who make their lives easier. Be one of them.

12. Embrace the Speed of Business

Business moves faster than you think. Early in your career, you'll feel like you're constantly being dragged behind a truck. That's normal. You won't have all the answers, and you won't always feel ready. You're sharpening your skills, which is an important part of the journey.

Don't try to slow the game down to your comfort level. Rise to the speed of business. Struggle *now* so you can master it sooner. Every skill worth having feels too fast before it becomes natural.

A Final Word

You've got your whole career ahead of you, and you don't need to be perfect to make it a good one. What you *do* need is the willingness to work and to learn. Be humble, step up, and stay out of the weeds. These best practices will help you build a life and career you can be proud of.

Remember the Dirty Dozen. Carry them with you and use them. When the day comes that you look back on the early years of your career, you'll be able to say with a full heart, "I'm glad I did."

Now go do something for the cause of good today.

—Mel

Conclusion

Thank you for taking this ride through the wild west of business with me. You've seen what it really takes to fix a culture, protect your people, and build something worth handing down. Now it's time to saddle up and hit the trail on your own.

Your people want to know what's in this for them. Each one is walking around holding a sign that says, "Make me feel special." How you treat and inspire them makes all the difference in whether they show up as their best or their worst. The uncommon sense you've learned in this book is the formula that will help you lead your people from mediocrity to excellence.

Traction, leverage, and empowerment in your organization create a foothold that stirs the hearts, minds, and souls of the individuals who make up your departments and teams. Leaders must be good shepherds who stir the souls of humans. Many leaders never figure that out.

Best practice is transformational, but a company made up of people being their worst selves is an illogical environment for best practice. The Best Pledge using the self-selves-team-teams approach is the real secret to traction. Best practice requires each person operating as the best versions of themselves.

Weaving together a group of men and women who commit to be their best selves and do their best work as a team is the epicenter of traction and leverage in any organization. Through every story, scar, and Mel-ism in this book, I've shown you how to build a strong workplace culture from the top down and back up again. This is how you fix what's broken and build something wonderful. Following what I've laid out here will help you—the good guy—win.

Every waking morning, an uncommon sense inspires a culture that lifts people and cultures to excellence. These principles work. They've been tested in the field, not just in a classroom.

Your Journey Through the Wild West

How about a quick recap? We've covered a lot of ground together in this book, and looking back will show you how very far you've come since you first cracked it open and started to read.

We started our journey by defining the difference between a company that's barely surviving and one that's thriving in the wild west of business. You learned how to identify and smooth out those square-wheeled wagons so you can gain and maintain momentum no matter what's going on in the industry or economy.

I showed you how to create a culture that stops worshiping problems and starts solving them. You also learned how to set up a weekly meeting pulse that keeps your people on task and fired up. No more drive-by meetings that do nothing but push problems up!

You now know how to identify the rattlesnakes and culture bandits that poison alignment—and how to deal with them quickly and cleanly before they can harm the business.

You've seen that true leaders aren't timid. They're gunslingers who are steady and decisive when the moment calls for it. You've discovered why structure first, people second is the *only* way to build a business that doesn't collapse under its own confusion. And you've realized that instead of asking cats to bark, the best thing to do is put the right people in the right seats.

You learned what it takes to build a Pony Up culture, where expectations are clear, accountability is normal, and every rider pulls their weight. You saw why fast fail, fast fix is the only way to move at the speed of business and why if you're not wrecking, you're not riding.

You learned why being the last good guy in the room means never putting down your gun, never ducking the responsibility to protect your culture, and never sacrificing integrity when the moment feels uncomfortable.

You've been given tools, strategies, stories, and straight talk from the trenches. Now you know what uncommon sense really looks like in action.

What Fixing Your Culture Requires

If you apply what's in this book, you'll fix your culture sooner than you expect. And all it takes is doing the simple, practical, no-nonsense things most leaders are too scared, too distracted, or too prideful to do. Things like:

- Building structure
- Killing chaos
- Creating clarity
- Protecting your people from culture bandits
- Solving real problems
- Holding your gun when everyone else puts theirs down
- Insisting on the best from yourself first, then others

This is how you begin to create something great. When you take action to do the above, momentum starts to build. That group of ordinary people you've been leading become a team worth following. And your organization starts winning consistently in a way that your competitors don't understand.

So it's your turn. No matter what your role in your company is, you can lead from right where you are today. You don't have to wait for permission or a high-powered title. And you definitely don't have to wait for the perfect conditions.

You have everything you need to walk into your workplace tomorrow and start applying uncommon sense. Start small if you have to. Pick one concept and start putting it to work. You've plenty to choose from:

- Worshiping the Problem
- Drive-By Meetings
- Keeping the Rattler out of the Baby's Crib
- Square-Wheeled Wagons
- Structure First, People Second
- Fast Fail, Fast Fix

- Stop Asking Cats to Bark
- The Best Pledge

If you have a team, explain it to your team as you model it yourself. Then repeat, protect, and enforce it. Cultures don't transform until the people inside them do. And it starts with you! Leaders transform cultures one decision, one standard, and one courageous moment at a time.

If This Resonated With You…

Uncommon sense requires "taking care of things" in implementation. Uncommon sense requires embracing these tried and true best practices as well as the logical and required chronological order in which to implement them. Both of these build and create momentum if done with care but create chaos if handled with malpractice.

Want help embedding uncommon sense deep in your business? If these straight-shooting strategies resonate with you, and you're ready to transform your culture, build a problem-solving organization, deepen your leadership, or sharpen your executive team, we should talk.

I speak, teach, coach senior teams, and consult. I work with organizations ready to fix what's broken to build something strong enough to last. If you want me to help you, your team, or your entire company put these principles into practice, you can book a call with me to talk about what would be a good fit for you. Visit the resource section of this book for a link to my calendar.

Final Words

Thank you for taking this ride with me. Now go lead. Go fix your workplace culture and protect the people counting on you. Be the good guy or gal who never puts down their gun. When you do, you'll build something people talk about and are proud to be a part of.

All it takes is a little uncommon sense.

Resources

Book a Call

Want help embedding uncommon sense deep in your business? If these straight-shooting strategies resonate with you and you're ready to transform your culture, build a problem-solving organization, deepen your leadership, or sharpen your executive team, we should talk. Scan the QR code below to schedule a discovery call.

Access Book Resources

Access the resources mentioned in this book, including:

- An org chart template
- The Razor™ Training

Visit the resource page of my website at https://www. MelBlackwell.com/resources or scan the QR Code below:

Other Resources

Stay up-to-date on what's going on in the business leadership world by tuning in to my podcast, *The Mel Blackwell Experience Podcast*: https://www.MelBlackwell.com/podcast

Acknowledgements

First and foremost, I'd like to thank my wife and partner in life, Gwen Blackwell. She carries the scars of learning uncommon sense right alongside me and has remained my number one fan through it all. She loves me, and I don't take for granted the kind of support I have at home. Gwen, I literally could not have accomplished what I have without you.

To Willis Potts, my stepfather. He came into our lives at a time when my mom and I really needed him. I'm so grateful he stepped up to be a dad to a 15-year-old kid when he didn't have to.

To Art Williams, the man who built an empire teaching leadership through satellite television. He opened my eyes to culture and what a culture leader really does when I was just a wet-behind-the-ears young man. He is the reason I wandered down this trail in the first place, and he's the reason I'm so committed to championing healthy business culture.

I'd also like to thank the professionals who believed in me and taught me so much throughout my career. Your support, encouragement, and insight during our years working together was invaluable:

- Trent Tetterton and Scott Ross at Actel

- Phil Lombardo, Jamie Ferguson, Mark Roth, Brian Cook, and Stan Sech, my bosses and mentors at USA Mobile
- Tom McLeod and Rick Halbrooks of McLeod Software
- Jim Stephens and Tim Collins at EBSCO

Thank you. Before I knew who I could become, you saw my potential and nurtured it.

I also want to thank James Leitner for introducing me to Ken DeWitt.

Last but definitely not least, I'd like to thank Gino Wickman and Ken DeWitt from Entrepreneur Operating System (EOS). You created a brilliant working business system. It's been my honor to expand on implementing it through *Uncommon Sense*.